♥ ♥ ♥

The

♥♥Life

Tastes Better Than

Steak♥♥

EATING PLAN

♥ ♥ ♥

A Diet for a Clogged Artery

by Gerry Krag, MA, RD

♥ ♥ ♥

While the information in this book may be beneficial to heart patients, it is not to be interpreted as medical advice or consultation for any specific condition.

No portion of this publication may be reproduced, reprinted or otherwise copied for distribution purposes without the express written permission of the author and publisher.

ISBN #0-932212-96-4
Library of Congress Catalog #97-073103

Copyright ©1997 by

Avery Color Studios
Marquette, Michigan

and

Gerry Krag, MA, RD

Printed by Lake Superior Press
Marquette, Michigan

♥ ♥ ♥

While we have made every effort to be accurate, the nutrient calculations in this book cannot be guaranteed. Because ingredients and nutritional content of prepared and processed foods are sometimes modified over time, the fat grams may vary.

♥ ♥ ♥

The Progressive Nature of Heart Disease

Coronary artery disease is progressive. If you do nothing, it will get worse. Medications may slow it down. Bypass surgery and angioplasty improve symptoms and may save lives, but are not permanent solutions. Blockages usually return after both procedures.

Changing behavior works. Eating extremely low-fat foods, exercising and learning to become peaceful and relaxed are more effective than any procedure or medication. Understanding the progressive nature of heart disease helps patients to change their behavior. Feeling better helps people stick to behavior changes.

Since 1992, I have had the privilege of working with a large group of people who are reversing their heart disease. Ordinary people with heart disease who made the lifestyle changes necessary to improve the blood flow to their hearts. These people never thought they would become vegetarians. Now they are committed vegetarians with healthier hearts. With effort and determination, you can accomplish this, too.

If you think your doctor can cure you with a pill or a procedure, The *"Life Tastes Better Than Steak"* Eating Plan is not for you. Pills and procedures can be a beneficial part of caring for your disease, but they will not cure it.

If you think you can reverse coronary blockages and still use low-fat milk and red meat, The *"Life Tastes Better Than*

♥ ♥ ♥

Steak" *Eating Plan* is not for you. A complete break from fat is necessary.

If you have reached a point in your life and are ready for MAJOR changes, keep reading. *The **"Life Tastes Better Than Steak"** Eating Plan* is ready and waiting for you.

> Yours in health,
> Gerry Krag, MA, RD
> 1997

Special Note:

*The **"Life Tastes Better Than Steak"** Eating Plan* would not be possible without the helpfulness of the caring patients and staff members of the Downriver Reversal Team. Many lent a hand with the editing of the fat grams and provided insights and suggestions. Thanks are also due to Nancy Kennedy, MA, RD, and Marie Zimolzak, DTR, for their assistance and to the always-helpful staff at Avery Color Studios. I am especially indebted to the support and enthusiasm of Dr. Joseph C. Rogers whose pioneering spirit is behind the success of the Downriver Reversal Team. The encouragement and love of my husband, Mike, has helped sustain this project from the beginning.

♥ ♥ ♥

Can I Really Heal My Heart ?

The good news is YES — it is possible to reverse your coronary artery disease. It is not easy and it won't happen overnight, but if you are committed, it can happen. Nearly ninety percent of the people using The **"Life Tastes Better Than Steak"** *Eating Plan* in conjunction with exercise, group support and yoga classes, have improved or stabilized their heart disease. For some, it happened in six months. For others, it took as long as two years. Those who are more serious do better than those who go about it in a halfhearted way. Women seem to have an easier time reversing their heart disease; but men have great success, too. If you would like to go ahead, follow these steps in the reversal process:

1. Read Dr. Dean Ornish's Program For Reversing Heart Disease, (Bantam, $6.95). This is the ground breaking book that describes the process of reversal. Dr. Ornish is the first scientist to demonstrate reversal through lifestyle changes. His book is full of information on all aspects of reversal: yoga, stress management, food intake, and exercise.

2. See a cardiologist regularly who will monitor your progress with checkups and tests. If you are a heart patient and you are not seeing a cardiologist, you are not taking care of your-

self properly. You are not being fair to yourself and to those close to you. Make sure you are being followed medically.

3. Seek out kindred spirits. Find a group of people who share your interest in reversing their own heart disease. A support group will make the lifestyle changes go smoother for you. Learn to share your feelings and open up within a support group. Patients, who try without the support group, find the changes much more difficult to make. A support group can originate through a church, hospital, worksite, or other community-based organization.

4. Get regular aerobic exercise. Work with your doctor and an exercise physiologist to develop an exercise prescription that is individualized for you. It helps to exercise with supportive people; you will be more conscientious with a group.

5. Join a yoga class and enjoy the benefits of stretching, balance exercise, deep relaxation and meditation. Like exercise, it helps to take yoga with friends or supportive people .

6. Work with a registered dietitian using The *"Life Tastes Better Than Steak" Eating Plan* as a guide. Work together as a team. The first few weeks are the most difficult, and it

is much easier if you share the inevitable ups and downs. Don't expect your dietitian to "shape you up". You will need to develop skills and confidence in following The *"Life Tastes Better Than Steak" Eating Plan*, so that eventually you can follow the plan independently. Your dietitian will offer you support, encouragement, and instruction; but you will have to do the rest. A registered dietitian has the skills and training to determine if you are eating correctly and can teach you how to assess your food intake for nutritional adequacy. For a registered dietitian near you, call 1-800-366-1655.

7. As the weeks and months pass, the lifestyle changes you have made will become your preference. You will be motivated to continue *because you feel better*.

♥ ♥ ♥

What Is The
"Life Tastes Better Than Steak"
Eating Plan?

The **"Life Tastes Better Than Steak"** *Eating Plan* is a simple vegetarian diet. No meat, poultry, or fish are eaten. It is also a "no added fat" program. No oils, including olive, peanut or canola oil are used. Foods that have added oils are not eaten. For example, tabouli salad prepared the traditional way is not eaten because it is prepared with a significant amount of olive oil. Tabouli salad prepared without olive oil is acceptable since there is no added fat. Nuts or seeds are not eaten, except a small amount for garnish, occasionally. Dairy foods with fat such as cheese and milk are not eaten, but nonfat dairy foods are used. Egg yolks are not used, but egg whites and fat free egg substitutes may be eaten freely. Vegetable oil cooking spray is used, but sparingly.

You can eat a variety of foods and be well nourished. Most people find they can eat a fair amount of food and not gain weight. If you are following the eating plan the right way, you should not experience excess hunger. You may need to snack between meals because low-fat foods move through the digestive tract quickly.

Besides lowering fat intake, about 30 percent of people with heart disease need to modify sodium intake. Some patients need to watch excess sugars and calories to prevent triglycerides or weight from rising. All will benefit by giving up caffeine. Caffeine can cause problems for those with irregular

♥ ♥ ♥

Bypasses Deliver Blood Around Blockages

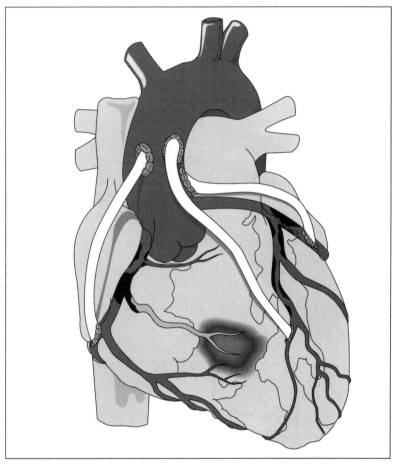

*Bypasses are sewn to the great aorta and deliver blood to the coronary arteries, "bypassing" blockages. Many bypass operations last less than ten years, even on a 30% fat diet. With intense lifestyle changes and following The **Life Tastes Better Than Steak** Eating Plan, heart patients have prevented blockages from recurring and have demonstrated improved heart function.*

♥ ♥ ♥

ABC's of *The "Life Tastes Better Than Steak" Eating Plan*

A. Fat gram intake of 10 - 13 grams per day

B. Vegetarian eating — no meat, poultry, fish

C. No added fats — fat or oil is not added to any food

D. Higher fat foods are not used — egg yolks, regular cheese, low fat cheese, nuts, whole milk, low fat milk, seeds, avocado, olives

E. No "Fat Free" foods with fat in the ingredients e.g., whipped topping mix or dairy creamers

Use These Foods Daily:

A. Fat free dairy foods

B. Fat free egg substitutes and egg whites

C. Fat free meat substitutes such as soy burgers, textured soy nuggets, and wheat gluten products such as seitan*

D. Fat reduced tofu and other fermented soy products such as miso*

*higher sodium food

♥ ♥ ♥

E. Dried beans and peas

F. Breads, cereals, pasta, starches

G. Vegetables and fruits

Use these for sauces, gravies, and seasoning to enhance flavor and prevent foods from sticking to cookware:

A. Fat free vegetable broth

B. Fat free meat-based broth (refrigerate and remove all traces of fat)

C. Herbs and seasonings

D. Fat free butter flavored sprinkles

E. Vegetable oil cooking spray (use sparingly; contains fat)

♥ ♥ ♥

The Pain of Angina

Not all heart patients have angina or chest pain. For those who do, angina varies from person to person. Some have classical chest pain, while others have pressure or radiating pain to the arm, back, neck or jaw. Keeping track of the number of episodes is important information to report to your doctor. Some causes for angina include stress, cigarettes, overexertion, competitive exercise, and binges of high fat food. Angina patients following The **"Life Tastes Better Than Steak"** *Eating Plan with exercise and other lifestyle changes have reduced their episodes dramatically. Having less angina provides motivation to eat less fat.*

♥ ♥ ♥

WARNING! Three Important Concerns

1. When following *The **"Life Tastes Better Than Steak"** Eating Plan* together with regular exercise and stress management, patients report they have more energy and less chest pain. Even if you feel better, you must use caution with vigorous exercise, competitive exercise, or difficult physical tasks. Learn to ask for help for the bigger jobs like moving furniture. Don't compete against computer games in exercise equipment. Avoid challenges like competitive basketball or other sports. Don't overdo it in the garden. Remember to take care of yourself. ***Protect yourself from over-doing.***

2. Once your body gets used to a very low-fat intake, the amount of bile you produce will decrease. Bile is produced by the liver and is stored in the gall bladder. The gall bladder is like a small bottle of liquid soap. When fat is

Is a steak worth it?

present in the small intestine, the gall bladder will release bile to "soap" up the fat. Fat is then absorbed through the intestinal wall and into the lymphatic system. (If your gall bladder has been removed, you will pass bile directly from the liver into the intestine.)

Your liver will produce enough bile to process the fat that you eat each day, plus a little extra. Suppose you are used to eating 12 fat grams per day. What happens when you go to your niece's wedding and eat 70 fat grams? The first 12 or so fat grams will mix with bile and easily pass through. The remaining fat grams will be left in the small intestine, waiting for bile which eventually recirculates via the liver back to the gall bladder. As those fat grams sit in your intestine, they may cause some gas-like symptoms. You may experience a bloated, full feeling lasting several hours. Most people who have experienced this agree that it was not worth the fat they ate. An experience like this can be a painful reminder that you have fallen off the wagon. **Protect yourself from fat.**

3. Research has shown that a single episode of high fat eating may cause arteries to spasm and blood to clot easier. For some people with blocked arteries, one binge of fat can lead to an angina episode. Many heart patients have found themselves in the emergency room after an evening of high fat foods. More heart problems occur around birthdays and holidays than at other times. **Protect yourself from fat.**

♥ ♥ ♥

What Can I Eat?

PLENTY!

There are many fat free foods available such as soy meat substitutes, egg substitutes, fat free dairy foods, fat free sauces and fat free dressings. Use along with vegetables, fruit, whole grain cereals, breads, rice and pasta to provide variety and flavor to your meals.

Soy burger and roasted potato slices

♥ A typical breakfast is grapefruit, hot cereal, some skim milk, and bagel with jam.

♥ A typical lunch is a bowl of fat free soup, a "Boca Burger™" (meatless, fat free burger), a fat free bun, roasted potato slices, a mixed green salad with fat free dressing, a glass of skim milk.

♥ A typical snack is fat free yogurt sweetened with a little fruit.

♥ A typical dinner is a stew made out of red beans, rice, and vegetables, a salad with fat free dressing, fat free bread or rolls, several steamed vegetables, and strawberries with fat free frozen yogurt for dessert.

♥ Try some of the many delicious recipes found in *The "Life Tastes Better Than Steak" Cookbook*, available from Avery Color Studios, Marquette, Michigan, 1-800-722-9925.

♥ ♥ ♥

Vegetarian Foods Are Not Always Lowfat

Vegetarian Lasagna: typical vegetarian lasagna prepared in a restaurant will have about 10-35 fat grams for a 3 inch square. Not a good choice if you want to reverse your heart disease.

Cheese Burritos: a cheese and bean burrito prepared in a restaurant will have about 11 fat grams. Not a good choice if you want to reverse your heart disease.

Marinara Sauce: meatless marinara prepared the traditional way in a restaurant will have anywhere from 3 to 19 fat grams. Not a good choice if you want to reverse your heart disease.

Fettuccini Alfredo: a one cup serving has about 28 fat grams. Not a good choice if you want to reverse your heart disease.

Watch out for these higher fat foods, unless you know they have been prepared without fat.

♥ ♥ ♥

Counting Fat Grams

The most successful way to decrease your fat intake is to count fat grams. Following a fat gram budget and counting your grams each day will teach you a lot about the amount of fats in foods. One fat gram is about one-fourth teaspoon of fat.

The process of learning how to count fat grams takes several weeks and to become skilled, you will need 8-12 weeks of practice. The best way to do this is to write down the food you eat and look up the amount of fat in each food *as you eat it*. Keeping a food record is critical to your success.

Heart patients often feel they have cut back on fats, and are surprised at the amount of fat they are eating when they keep a food record. There are many hidden fats in foods and you will find them when you keep a food record and you will miss them if you don't.

Failure to keep a food record is like going on a shopping spree without keeping track of your check writing—it's so easy to get overdrawn!!

The goal in counting fat grams is to learn how to eat in a measured low-fat way. Counting grams is the tool. Eventually you will have many fat grams "put to memory" and you won't have to keep looking up foods. After several weeks, you will automatically eat in a measured, low-fat way. Gradually, counting fat grams will become a habit. In time, this way of eating will become your preference. You will be motivated because you feel better. High fat foods will lose their appeal, as you find many delicious low-fat foods to replace them.

Your Food Record

Use your food record to write down the foods you eat. Look up the foods in the fat gram counter or on a food label. Write down the number of grams for all foods eaten. Copy and use the forms on pages 78 and 79. Keep tabs on your fat grams as you go through the day. If you are try-
ing to lose weight, your food record will be a powerful tool. The more food records you keep, the more success you will have. (See example on the following page).

Expect to make mistakes. You will learn from them. Be gentle with yourself when you make mistakes! For example, you may order Fettuccini Alfredo, thinking it is a vegetarian dish. Don't faint when you find out it has 28 fat grams from the cream and butter.

Your body needs about 8 - 12 fat grams each day. When you are eating vegetarian foods with no added fats, your fat intake will be about 10 -13 fat grams each day. However, you must make an effort to eat lots of vegetables, whole grain foods, dried

beans, and good sources of protein. Without these foods, your fat intake will be too low. Keeping a food record will help you to eat in a healthy way and get the fat you need. Too little fat or protein is not healthy.

♥ ♥ ♥

Your Food Record

DAY ___	DAILY FAT GRAM GOAL 10-13		DAILY FAT GRAM TOTAL 10.4
TIME	**FOOD**	**Amount**	**Fat Gm.**
8 am	skim milk	1 c.	0.4
	oatmeal	1 c.	2.0
	banana	1	0.6
	toast—fat free bread	1	0.0
	orange juice	1/2 c.	0.0
10 am	bagel (frozen)	1	1.0
	cream cheese, fat free	2 tbs	trace
12:30 pm	egg salad sandwich:		
	wheat bread, fat free	2	0.0
	mayo, fat free	4 tbs	0.0
	lettuce, relish, onion		0.0
	egg whites, boiled	2	0.0
	tomato slices	3	0.0
	three bean salad	1-1/2 c	3.0
	herb tea		0.0
2:45 pm	pear	1	0.7
5:30 pm	mixed green salad	2 c.	0.3
	dressing, fat free	2 tbs	0.0
	pasta	1 c.	1.0
	marinara sauce (no added fat)	1 c.	0.0
	textured soy protein	3 tbs	0.0
	sweet potato	1 c.	1.0
	skim milk	1 c.	0.4

Keep tabs on your fat grams as you go through the day. If you are trying to lose weight, your food record will be a powerful tool.

♥ ♥ ♥

Doesn't My Body Need Some Fat?

Yes, your body needs fat — about 8-12 fat grams every day. This fat can be supplied through vegetable sources. Your body will use this fat in the following ways:

1. To keep skin nourished and healthy.

2. To maintain the layer of fat just under the skin that insulates and stabilizes body temperature.

3. To transport and absorb the fat soluble vitamins A,D,E, and K.

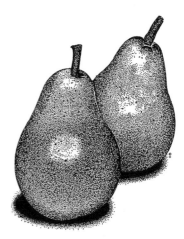

4. To maintain the membrane around cells, a fatty layer that protects cells from invaders, such as viruses and bacteria.

5. To maintain the fatty cushion around organs such as the heart and kidneys. This fat absorbs shock.

6. To replenish the bile acids which are used to help absorb fat into your system.

Because The **"Life Tastes Better Than Steak"** Eating Plan uses no added fat, you may wonder where you are going to get the fat that you need every day. If you are eating a variety of foods, you should be able to obtain enough fat each day. Consider the following healthy foods:

The "Life Tastes Better Than Steak" Eating Plan

♥ ♥ ♥

FOOD	AMOUNT	FAT GRAMS
most whole grain cereals	1 cup	0.5 - 1.0
oatmeal	1 cup, cooked	1.8
garbanzo beans	1 cup, cooked	4.2
most dried beans	1 cup, cooked	2.0
pasta	1 cup, cooked	1.0
rice, brown	1 cup	1.8
many breads	1 slice	1.0
vegetable oil cooking spray	1 second spray	1.0
tofu, light, silken	6 oz.	2.0
most vegetables	1 cup	0.2-0.4
corn	1 cup	2.2
green limas	1 cup	0.7
winter squash	1 cup	1.2
sweet potato	1 cup	1.0
tomato paste	1/2 cup	1.2
most fruits	1 serving	0.2-0.4
banana	1 medium	0.6
pear	1 medium	0.7
pineapple	1 cup	0.7
most berries	1 cup	0.6-0.7
whole wheat flour	1 cup	2.4
whole grain corn meal	1 cup	4.6
vitamin E	800 I.U.	0.8

♥ ♥ ♥

Why Can't I Eat Olive Oil?

The question about using olive oil is asked by almost every heart patient. If olive oil helps prevent heart disease in Mediterranean countries, why can't I use it? The answer is in the word **PREVENT**. Olive oil and other monounsaturated fats are beneficial in preventing  heart disease, but what if you already have blocked arteries? Is there any evidence that olive oil will help open your blocked arteries? To date, there is no evidence that olive oil or other monounsaturated fats can reverse heart disease. Heavy use of these liquid fats is detrimental to anyone with blocked arteries.

Fats can be divided into three categories: saturated, polyunsaturated, and monounsaturated. Saturated fats are the most dangerous for heart patients because they go to the liver and are processed into cholesterol. Saturated fat is found in animal-based fat, hydrogenated fat and tropical fat (palm and coconut oil).

Polyunsaturated fat is oil made from crops such as corn, safflower, soy, sunflower, and cotton. Polyunsaturated fat is often saturated with hydrogen to make margarine and shortening. As an oil, polyunsaturated fat can help lower cholesterol, but it will also lower your good cholesterol. It is no longer a recommended choice for heart patients. In addition, both saturated and polyunsaturated fat can oxidize in the blood and damage the inner lining of your arteries.

The third kind of fat, monounsaturated fat, lowers your cholesterol level without lowering your good cholesterol. Monounsaturated fat does not oxidize. The three most common monounsaturated fats are olive oil, canola oil, and peanut oil. For someone trying to prevent heart disease, these can be beneficial. But for someone with blockages, they may cause problems because these oils are not 100 percent pure monounsaturated fat.

So, What's Wrong With Olive Oil?

Take a look at these monounsaturated fats:

One tablespoon of:

Olive oil = 14 grams total fat
      saturated fat: . . . . 2 grams*
      polyunsaturated fat: . . . . . 1 gram*
      monounsaturated fat: . . . . 11 grams*

Canola oil = 14 grams of total fat
      saturated fat: . . . . 1 gram*
      polyunsaturated fat: . . . . . 4 grams*
      monounsaturated fat: . . . . 9 grams*

Peanut oil = 14 grams of total fat
      saturated fat: . . . . 2 grams*
      polyunsaturated fat: . . . . . 4 grams*
      monounsaturated fat: . . . . 8 grams*

All oils have 12-14 fat grams in each tablespoon.

actual fat grams vary slightly among brands

If you eat a tablespoon of olive oil on pasta and another one on a salad, you will consume 28 fat grams and four of them will be saturated fat. This is equivalent to one teaspoon of saturated fat. If you have blockages in your coronary arteries, this teaspoon of saturated fat will not help, and could make the situation worse. Using monounsaturated fats in sprays to prevent sticking is one way of using them without getting much saturated fat. One second of the spray is about one fat gram.

Eating nuts and avocados will also contribute to your saturated fat intake. These foods may be beneficial for preventing heart disease in healthy people, but they have not proven to reverse existing blockages and are not recommended.

♥ ♥ ♥

What? No Chicken or Fish?

Counting your cholesterol intake is a waste of time and does not work. Here is why: cholesterol is measured in milligrams. A tenth of a liter of blood is used to measure your cholesterol count. A 150 pound person with a cholesterol count of 200 will have approximately 10,000 milligrams of cholesterol flowing in the blood at a given time. If that person eats a food with 50 milligrams (mg) of cholesterol, it will be adding 50 mg to the total 10,000 milligrams. This is only a drop in the bucket.

Fat is measured in grams. Each gram is equal to 1000 milligrams. Most of your cholesterol is manufactured from saturated and hydrogenated fat. If you produce cholesterol easily (and most heart patients do) you will make significant amounts of cholesterol from each gram of saturated or hydrogenated fat that you eat. Each gram of saturated fat that you eat has the potential of producing hundreds of milligrams of cholesterol. This represents a significant amount.

A 10 1/2 ounce broiled, trimmed beef steak has the potential of adding thousands of milligrams of cholesterol to your blood, all at one time! A one ounce slice of cheese has the potential of adding thousands of milligrams of cholesterol into your blood. In heart patients, excess cholesterol will quickly become deposited into tissues and artery walls. It will also oxidize and damage the artery wall. Patients with blocked arteries who continue to eat foods with saturated fat will continue to build blockages. Patients who give up saturated fat and become vegetarians do better than those who continue to eat even lean poultry and fish. The bottom line is that eating small portions of very lean chicken and fish every day has the potential of adding thousands of milligrams of cholesterol to your blood each week*. If you have blocked arteries, this is too much cholesterol.

In addition to cholesterol coming from saturated fat, cholesterol is produced by the extra calories you eat that are not burned off as energy or stored as body fat. Fat free foods are not always low in calories. Work on maintaining a healthy weight to prevent extra calories from being manufactured into cholesterol and fat.

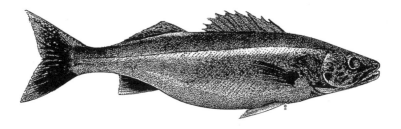

*A three ounce portion of skinless chicken breast has three fat grams, one of which is saturated. If you eat three or four chicken breasts each week, it could add three or four saturated fat grams into your liver. If you are a person who produces a lot of cholesterol, your liver could manufacture thousands of milligrams of cholesterol from the chicken each week. A three ounce portion of salmon has three fat grams, one of which is saturated. If you have three or four small pieces of salmon a week, you would add three or four more saturated fat grams into your liver. This could produce thousands of milligrams of cholesterol each week.

♥ ♥ ♥

Shopping For Food

Believe it or not, shopping for low-fat foods can be much faster than shopping for traditional foods. There are whole areas of the store that you need not even walk through. An example is the meat counter. No meat to buy, fewer decisions to make.

Following the **no added fat** protocol makes shopping faster as well. There are many foods that are fat free. Study the labels and find the ones you like; once you do, shopping goes faster.

Schedule some time to do your **shopping homework**, i.e., a time when you can scan through the store without a deadline, reading labels and examining foods. The best time to do this is early morning or late at night. Stores are less crowded then, and you won't be in the way of other shoppers. Avoid shopping when you are hungry, extra tired, or stressed out.

A full service grocery store will have many products such as fat free breads and dairy foods. Health food stores will have specialty items such as fat free "Boca Burgers™" and other meat substitutes. Produce markets are excellent sources for fruits and vegetables.

Consider using organically grown produce when available. You will be increasing the amount of produce you eat, so you might as well eat the purest you can find. Food co-ops may be good sources of organically grown food.

As you shop, focus on the fat free foods that you like. Don't buy foods just because they are fat free. Manufacturers are rushing fat free foods to the marketplace, some better than others.

Read both the nutrition label for the fat grams and the ingredient list for added fats. It is legal for a fat free product to have less than .5 fat grams per serving.

For example a "fat free" coffee creamer could have .4 fat grams of hydrogenated soy bean oil per tablespoon. If you poured a cup of this on your cereal, you would consume sixteen tablespoons of the creamer for a total of 6.4 fat grams. Use skim milk or fat free soy milk instead. Always check the ingredient list for added fat.

Fat Free Foods Are Not Always Fat Free

Many foods in the grocery store are listed as fat free, yet they contain added fat. How can you identify these foods? Make a point to read the ingredient list and look for fats or fatty foods in the list. *If fat is in the ingredient list, count "fat free" foods as .4 grams per serving*. Avoid these foods.*

*The actual amount may vary from 0.1 - 0.4 grams

Avoid fat free foods with "fat" in the ingredient list.

♥ ♥ ♥

Fat free foods that contain coconut oil, palm oil, hydrogenated oil, and animal fat are particularly important to avoid. Look for words like:

butter	safflower oil	partially hydrogenated oil
lard	canola oil	coconut oil
cream	rapeseed oil	tahina
sweet cream	olive oil	nut butter
cheese	cottonseed oil	nuts
whole milk	sesame oil	whole eggs
lowfat milk	palm oil	monoglycerides
buttermilk	peanut oil	diglycerides
meat fat	vegetable oil	
meat	hydrogenated oil, any kind	
corn oil		

Labels and Ingredients

The nutrition label will help you find foods that are fat free or low fat. However, the label was designed for healthy people and conforms to the guideline of 30% of calories coming from fat. The **"Life Tastes Better Than Steak"** *Eating Plan* was designed for cardiac patients and is based on less than 10% of calories coming from fat. The nutritional guidelines at the bottom of the label and the percentage recommendations on the right side of the food label are inappropriate for someone who wishes to reverse heart disease. For example, if you are a healthy person eating about 2000 calories each day, the bottom of the food label recommends 65 fat grams per day. Refer to the sample label on the next page:

Refer to the Nutrition Label on Foods

The information on this side of the label will help you find low fat and fat free food. The fat grams are listed after the words "total fat."

Saturated fat is the most dangerous for heart patients.

Most fat free and low fat foods are also low in cholesterol.

A good level for sodium is under 2000 mg./day.

A good level for fiber is 20-35 grams/day.

Nutrition Facts
Serving Size 1/2 cup dry (43g)
Servings per container 11

Amount per Serving

Calories 148   Calories from Fat 0

	% Daily Value*
Total Fat 0g	**0%**
Saturated Fat 0g	**0%**
Cholesterol 0g	**0%**
Sodium 0mg	**0%**
Total Carbohydrate 14g	**5%**
Dietary Fiber 5g	**20%**
Sugars 1g	
Protein 23g	

Vitamin A	0%	•	Vitamin C	0%
Calcium	15%	•	Iron	35%
Magnesium	35%	•	Zinc	15%

• Percent Daily Values are based on a 2,000 calorie diet. Your daily values may be higher or lower depending on your calorie needs:

		2,000 Calories	2,500 Calories
Total Fat	Less than	65g	80g
Sat. Fat	Less than	20g	25g
Cholesterol	Less than	300mg	300mg
Sodium	Less than	2,400mg	2,400mg
Total Carbohydrate		300g	375g
Dietary Fiber		25g	30g

Calories per gram:
Fat 9 • Carbohydrate 4 * Protein 4

Serving size and servings per container are important.

Do not add "total fat" and "saturated fat" together. Use total fat for food record.

% Daily Values were developed for healthy people. Ignore these.

Ingredients list: items are listed by volume. Fat has not been added to this list.

Ingredients: Textured Vegetable Protein from defatted soybeans.

♥ ♥ ♥

What Can I Buy For Snacks?

Fat free and lowfat foods are digested and absorbed quickly. You may experience hunger between meals and healthy snacks will help you to maintain good blood sugar levels. Your body needs high quality snacks. Sweet snacks have many disadvantages: Sweets will not keep the hungries away. Sweets may cause your blood sugar to drop. Sweets probably will raise your triglycerides. Sweets are a concentrated source of calories and will interfere with weight loss.

Snacks will be more satisfying if they include both carbohydrate and protein. You will experience fewer food cravings if your snacks include good sources of protein, such as beans, soy foods, or fat free dairy foods. Many reversal patients have found that fat free soy lunchmeats make quick and tasty sandwiches that can be eaten between meals. Shakes made from blended fresh fruit and tofu are satisfying, filling, and surprisingly good.

Fruits are healthy snacks, but if you are eating too much fruit, the results may be similar to sweets. How much fruit is too much? This is a hard question to answer. If you are a diabetic or if you have high triglycerides, eat no more than four servings per day. Most patients can eat fruit freely, but those who eat eight or ten servings of fruit a day or drink several large glasses of fruit juice a day may find that weight loss goals are not met and that triglycerides are high. Who would eat that much? Many reversal patients in the first few weeks of the program often do. Frequent hunger, coupled with the convenience and good taste of fruit, leads to overeating. Fruit is an important food, but should not be over emphasized.

♥ ♥ ♥

Other suggestions:

- ♥ veggies and bean dip made from mashed beans, fat free mayo, onion and your favorite seasonings
- ♥ bean soup and fat free crackers
- ♥ fat free corn chips and fat free refried beans
- ♥ pizza made with pita bread, veggies, fat free cheese, and fat free soy pepperoni
- ♥ fat free cream cheese and a bagel half
- ♥ fat free pasta and bean salad
- ♥ plain fat free yogurt with shredded cucumber (seasoned with onion and garlic) over Romaine lettuce served with toasted or fresh pita bread
- ♥ fat free cheese and fat free crackers
- ♥ baked potato topped with steamed veggies and fat free cheese
- ♥ baked sweet potato
- ♥ skim milk and high fiber cereal, topped with fruit
- ♥ hot cereal prepared with skim milk
- ♥ skim milk shake made with fruit and fat free soy protein supplement
- ♥ fat free cottage cheese garnished with fruit or vegetables
- ♥ scrambled fat free egg substitute and toast
- ♥ a tall glass of water with a lemon wedge is great with snacks

♥ ♥ ♥

Shopping Strategies

You will spend less money on food when you follow The **"Life Tastes Better Than Steak"** Eating Plan. Even though some fat free products may be more expensive, your overall cost for food will be less when you become a vegetarian. Meat is the most expensive food in the store.

Remember the Latin phrase "Caveat Emptor"— *let the buyer beware.*

♥ Always buy the fresh vegetables that you like and will use.

♥ When fresh vegetables are not available, consider plain frozen.

♥ Stock up on non-perishable foods, especially when they are on sale.

♥ Take advantage of "cents-off" coupons for fat free foods.

♥ Shop for portable food that you can carry with you for lunches or breaks.

♥ If the ingredient list has so many additives it looks like a chemistry text book, avoid the product.

♥ ♥ ♥

Shopping List:

Dairy Case:
fruit juice
skim milk
fat free cottage
  cheese*
fat free sour cream
fat free yogurt
fat free ricotta
fat free cheese*
fat free tacos
burrito shells
eggs (for whites)
tofu
soy lunchmeats*
seitan*
fat free soy milk

Produce:
all fruits & vegetables
except avocado &
  olives

Dry Goods:
rice, white & brown
instant brown rice
pasta and noodles
(no traditional
kluski or fettuccine)
dried beans, all kinds:
  -black beans
  -blackeyes

-fava beans
-kidney beans
-lentils
-lima beans
-navy beans
-pinto beans
-red beans
-split peas
-etc.
popcorn, plain
cold cereals
hot cereals
bread, white & wheat
bagels
English muffins
French bread
fat free muffins*
rolls
pita bread
lavash bread
fat free crackers*
barley
oats
tapioca
soy burger
textured soy protein

Canned Goods:
canned dried beans*
garbanzo beans*
canned tomatoes*

low sodium broth*
(chill to remove fat)
tomato sauce*
salsa*
fat free soups*
Pritikin™ foods
Health Valley™ foods
applesauce
fruits in juice or water
vegetable juice*

Condiments:
fat free mayonnaise*
fat free salad
  dressing*
catsup*
mustard*
vinegar
low sodium soy
  sauce*
teriyaki sauce*

Baking Ingredients:
white flour
whole wheat flour
high gluten flour
sugar/honey
sugar substitutes
Molly McButter™
(continued)

higher sodium food

♥ ♥ ♥

molasses
canola oil spray
olive oil spray
seasonings
salt substitute
plain gelatin
fat free puddings
corn starch
yeast
baking powder*
baking soda*

Frozen Foods:

plain vegetables
bagels
bread dough
fat free frozen desserts
juices
fat free egg substitute

frozen fruit
soy burgers
vegetable burgers
wheat gluten meat
    substitute
fat free soy protein

Beverages:

skim milk
fruit juice
decaf coffee
decaf tea
herbal tea

Sweets and Treats

(these may not be appropriate for diabetics or those with high triglycerides)

dried fruits
angel food cake
fat free bars
fat free cookies
marshmallows
popsicles
Italian ices
jams
jellies
sweet relish
pretzels*
fat free cakes

*higher sodium food

♥ ♥ ♥

Cooking Without Fat

Cooking to reverse your heart disease doesn't have to be a chore. It can be faster than going to a fast food restaurant:

1. Rinse a can of your favorite beans.
2. Simmer with a can of low sodium stewed tomatoes.
3. Serve over pasta or quick cooking brown rice.

Of course, "a recipe is just a beginning" – use the recipe as a guide and personalize it based on your own preferences. In the above example, you could saute fresh garlic, onion, a zucchini and your favorite herbs in a little wine, and add that to the recipe. Plan ahead and prepare recipes that can be frozen to be eaten on busy days. The cookbook **Life Tastes Better Than Steak** can be a great resource for you and your family. Use the following tips to revise some of your favorite high fat recipes. Remember, "a recipe is just a beginning."

If the recipe calls for:	*Try this instead:*
deep fat frying	♥ bake or broil with a small amount of vegetable oil cooking spray
	♥ or poach in water or fat free broth
sauteing in oil	♥ saute in water, wine, or fat free broth
baking or braising in oil	♥ use cooking spray, nonstick pans, or parchment
marinating in oil	♥ use fat free dressing*, teriyaki sauce*, or sodium reduced soy sauce* diluted with a little water
dredging in melted butter	♥ use fat free butter substitute such as liquid Butter Buds

higher sodium food

♥ ♥ ♥

breading and frying

♥ use herb coating instead of breading, saute in a little cooking spray

♥ or spray breading coat with a little cooking spray and bake in medium oven

regular or low-fat cheese*

♥ leave out the cheese

♥ or use fat free cheese made from skim milk (don't use high temperatures with fat free cheese)

chocolate chips

♥ use raisins or other dried fruit (note: limit use of dried fruit with elevated triglycerides)

chocolate, unsweetened squares

♥ use 3 TBS. cocoa powder for each square

cottage cheese*

♥ use fat free cottage cheese made from skim milk

♥ If sodium is a problem, rinse cheese in cold water, drain and return to container with a little skim milk. If you are on severe sodium restriction, avoid cottage cheese.

cream

♥ use canned evaporated skim milk

cream cheese*

♥ use fat free yogurt that has been drained of excess fluid (use cheese cloth or coffee filter)

♥ try fat free cream cheese (some cannot be used for baking—refer to label instructions)

higher sodium food

♥ ♥ ♥

eggs

- ♥ use 2 egg whites for each egg
- ♥ or use fat free egg substitute—check the label, not all substitutes are fat free

frosting

- ♥ use fruit sauces, sweetened fat free yogurt, or sweetened drained fat free yogurt
- ♥ use "seven minute frosting"
- ♥ use a glaze made with 1 cup powdered sugar and a few tablespoons of skim milk

fat: butter, margarine lard, oil, shortening bacon grease

- ♥ for baking, use equal amount of applesauce (exceptions: pie crust, shortbread, biscuits)

- ♥ for cooking and roasting, use vegetable oil cooking spray sparingly. Each one second spray equals one fat gram.

mayonnaise

- ♥ use fat free yogurt or fat free mayonnaise

salad dressings*

- ♥ use fat free dressings*—home made or commercial
- ♥ or use lemon juice or vinegar
- ♥ in restaurants, ask for lemon or vinegar

salt*   *(if your doctor has recommended a low sodium diet)*

- ♥ reduce amount or eliminate
- ♥ use salt substitute, unless your doctor recommends against this.
- ♥ use more herbs and seasonings

higher sodium food

♥ ♥ ♥

salt*, continued

♥ use sodium free and reduced sodium foods, but watch the fat content of these products.

♥ refrigerate low sodium broth and skim off fat

sauces and gravies

♥ make sauces and gravies from fat free broth. If using canned broth, refrigerate and remove all traces of fat

sour cream

♥ use fat free yogurt or fat free sour cream

♥ or use fat free ricotta

sugar

♥ quantity can be reduced as much as 50%

♥ experiment with less

♥ Sweet and Low® and Sugar Twin® can be used in baking. Equal® (Nutra-sweet) cannot be used with high temperatures

nuts

♥ use chopped water chestnuts in quick breads and cakes

ground meat

♥ use fat free textured vegetable soy protein or fat free soy burger* (Some protein is higher in sodium; check the label)

*higher sodium food

Getting The Nutrients You Need

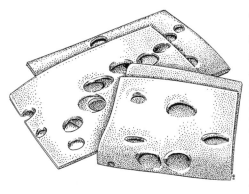

To make sure that you are getting the nutrients you need, compare your daily food intake to the Reversal Food Guide Pyramid. The number and sizes of servings for each of the food groups are listed. When your daily intake meets the recommended servings, your diet will be balanced and include most of the nutrients you need for health. Larger people will need more food than listed. Smaller people may need less.

In the beginning, the weakest areas for most people are inadequate protein and vegetables. It is one thing to give up meat, but if you do not replace the protein, you will not be properly nourished. We have found that heart patients who do not eat enough protein are frequently hungry, they experience food cravings, and they lack stamina.

Incorporating five servings of vegetables into your daily routine may take time and effort, but it is worth it. Vegetables have important nutrients and fiber. Heart patients who eat large amounts of fiber have fewer heart attacks. Eat more of the vegetables you like and can tolerate.

♥ ♥ ♥

Reversal Food Guide Pyramid

ALCOHOL, FAT FREE SWEETS AND TREATS
(recommended rarely)

FAT FREE DAIRY
(2 servings recommended)
1 cup skim milk
1 cup fat free yogurt
1 ounce fat free cheese*
1/2 cup fat free cottage cheese*
1/2 cup fat free ricotta
1 ounce fat free cream cheese*

PROTEIN
(2-4 servings recommended)
4 ounces of dried beans, cooked
4 egg whites (4 ounces or 1/2 c.)
4 ounces fat free egg substitute
4 ounces fat free meat substitute
4 ounces tofu or soy protein
2 tablespoons fat free soy powder protein supplement

FRUITS
(2-4 servings recommended)
1 medium raw fruit
1/2 large fruit
1 cup fresh fruit
1/2 cup sauce or juice
1/4 cup dried fruit

VEGETABLES
(5 or more servings recommended)
1 cup raw
1/2 cup cooked
1/2 cup vegetable juice*

BREADS/CEREALS/STARCHES
(6 or more servings recommended)
1 slice bread
1 medium potato
1 cup pasta, rice, or cereal
6 crackers*
1/2 bagel or English muffin
1 fat free tortilla

higher sodium food

Am I Getting Enough Protein?

It is normal to worry about protein intake when you first become a vegetarian. The best way to deal with this worry is to learn more about your protein needs and how to meet them. There are plenty of ways to get enough protein on a daily basis, even when you are not eating meat, fish, and poultry. A good rule of thumb is to eat 1-2 cups of cooked  legumes (dried beans and peas) and two servings of fat free dairy foods per day. There are other ways you can determine if you are getting enough protein. Just like fat, protein is measured in grams. Men over the age of 25 need about 63 grams each day; women over age 25 need about 50 grams. Older folks may need more. Use the chart on the next page and food labels to assess how many grams of protein you are eating daily.

In one day, if you had 2 cups of skim milk, 1 cup of cooked beans, 1 cup of pasta, 1 cup of cereal, 4 slices of bread, 5 servings of vegetables, and 2 egg whites, your protein would be about 70 grams. Your daily needs would have easily been met. There are many fat free meat substitutes available in your local health food stores. Remember to check the fat content and also the protein content before purchase.

FOOD AND SERVINGS	PROTEIN GRAMS
dried beans and peas (cooked), 1 cup	12-18
wheat gluten meat substitute, 4 ounces	19
fat free textured soy protein, 1/2 cup	23
fat free Boca Burger™, 1 patty	12
Fat reduced silken lite tofu, 6 ounces	10
fat free cottage cheese*, 1/2 cup	13
Lite-life™ or Yves™ fat free slices, 1 ounce	8-10
skim milk, 1 cup	8
fat free yogurt, 1 cup	8
Garden Veggie™, 1 patty	7
pasta, 1 cup	7
egg whites, 2 from large eggs	7
egg substitute, 1/4 cup	5
potato, 1 cup	6
fat free cheese, 1 ounce	6-9
rice, cooked, 1 cup	4
oatmeal, cooked, 1 cup	6
cold cereal, most hot cereal, 3/4 cup	3-4
bread, most kinds, 1 slice	3
vegetables, most, 1 /2 cup serving	2
fruits, 1 serving	0-2

*higher sodium food

❤ ❤ ❤

Taking Vitamin Supplements

A vegetarian diet can be very nutritious, and many vegetarians do not need to take supplements to get the vitamins and minerals necessary for health. To make sure your bases are covered, however, take a daily multiple vitamin. If you have trouble taking multiple vitamins, take an adult liquid vitamin, available from your pharmacist. Select a multiple vitamin that includes iron, vitamin B 12, and folic acid.

❤ Vitamin B 12 is found mostly in meats and dairy foods. If you are not eating fat free dairy foods and egg whites, your B 12 intake could be low.

❤ A small number of vegetarians may develop low iron, so taking iron in your multiple vitamin each day could be beneficial for you. "Senior" or "silver" vitamins often have less iron than adult vitamins. There is some evidence that a high level of iron in the blood is detrimental to heart patients. This has not been a problem for people following this eating plan.

❤ Folic acid is important for heart patients because it clears homocysteine from the blood. Elevated homocysteine, like cholesterol, is related to heart disease.

Some studies show that natural vitamins may be better absorbed, but research in this area is limited. Test your vitamin. It should dissolve in a small glass of water and one tablespoon vinegar within about twenty minutes.

♥ ♥ ♥

Oxidation and Antioxidant Vitamins

Oxidation is a common chemical reaction. A good example is rust, formed when steel is exposed to the atmosphere. We've all experienced the destructive nature of oxidation in our cars, lawn furniture, and other exposed items.

Fat can also oxidize. The most common fat to oxidize is LDL (lousy) cholesterol. When LDL cholesterol oxidizes, it irritates and damages the lining of our arteries. White blood cells then rush to the scene and push under the thin inner lining. These white blood cells begin to take on additional oxidized LDL cholesterol, forming fatty streaks within our arteries. Eventually, the buildup thickens, collects debris, and becomes known as plaque, which can restrict blood flow.

Plaque can build up in every artery, not just the ones in the heart. The arteries around the heart show the evidence of buildup because of their small size. Plaque often begins when we are children. For some people, a substantial amount can be laid down by age twenty. Women generally do not have significant build up until after menopause, but then they quickly catch up to men. People with risk factors tend to build up more plaque: family history, high blood pressure, lack of exercise, high cholesterol, and high fat intake. Smoking and stress both constrict arteries, making the disease worse. Smoke can also cause oxidative damage to the artery wall.

As plaque builds up, oxidation continues to be a danger. This is especially true if there is a lot of fat in the blood which may cause the tender inner lining of the artery to bleed. The blood pushes through the plaque causing "plaque rupture." The blood

♥ ♥ ♥

begins to clot, which blocks the artery. Plaque rupture can cause blood flow to become totally restricted, endangering the heart muscle. The coronary arteries are small. A clot the size of a pinhead can cause major problems. (See illustration on page 72.)

Preventing Oxidation

Your first line of defense against oxidation is to eat very little fat. More heart problems occur on holidays and birthdays than at any other time. Many patients report eating rich, fatty foods before their heart attack.

Your second line of defense is to take supplements of the anti-oxidant vitamins E and C. In many studies, people taking these two vitamins have had fewer coronary events.

♥ The recommended amount for vitamin E is
    400-800 I.U.'s. daily

♥ The recommended amount for vitamin C is
    100-500 mg. daily

Vitamin E is generally safe and easy to take. For best absorption, don't take vitamin E and your multiple vitamin at the same time of day and you need to take it with a meal. On a low fat diet, it is impossible to get 400 I.U.'s of vitamin E from dietary sources, since vitamin E is found mostly in oils, nuts, and seeds. Vitamin E is a mild blood thinner. If you are taking anticoagulents, discuss vitamin E with your doctor. Most patients can take vitamin E without problems. Preliminary research suggests that taking natural vitamin E (d-alpha-tocopherol) may be more effective than synthetic (dl-alpha-tocopherol).

Vitamin C is a safe vitamin for most people. However, a few precautions for vitamin C include:

1. Kidney patients should not take over 500 mg/day because it is hard for the kidneys to process excess amounts.

2. A very small number of people develop diarrhea with vitamin C levels over 500 mg.

3. If you are following a low sodium diet, purchase sodium free vitamin C.

To consume 100 mg. of vitamin C from food, you need to eat many sources everyday. Good sources include broccoli, bell peppers, melons, citrus, strawberries, kiwi fruits, tomatoes, cabbage, potatoes, pineapple, and greens.

♥ ♥ ♥

Vitamin A and Beta Carotene

Another important antioxidant is beta carotene. Your body uses beta carotene to make vitamin A. Taking too much vitamin A from supplements may cause health problems.

Beta carotene is a member of a larger group of carotenoids, most having antioxidant properties. The latest research indicates that the best way to get carotenoids is by eating fruits and vegetables, so carotenoids are in balance.

Aim for three or more servings each day of these foods:

carrots
sweet potato
tomatoes
leaf lettuce
cantaloupe
greens, all kinds
spinach
Romaine lettuce
peaches
iceberg lettuce
apricots
watermelon
pumpkins
nectarines

Chinese
　cabbage
winter squash
kale
broccoli
peppers, sweet
papaya

mango
grapefruit, pink
parsley
summer squash
peas
some enriched
　cereals

♥ ♥ ♥

The Dilemma of Eating Out and Socializing

At this time, most restaurants are not quite ready for reversal patients, although progress is being made. Soon you will see more low fat and fat free vegetarian entrees. Until that happens, you must have an action plan. Always ask for special consideration. For example, say "Could you please steam some vegetables for me?" Eating at a place where you know the chef/cook will help. Leaving a tip for the cook is a way of showing appreciation and has helped several people who eat often in the same restaurant. A great defense is to have some food before you go out, especially protein foods. This will help you feel less deprived and give you some fortitude. Hunger, coupled with the aroma of food, is a powerful "eating cue" that can wipe out resolve in seconds. If you are served a food you think might have added fat, press a bit of your napkin into the food. If a grease mark remains, the food has added fat. If a water mark remains, the food probably has little added fat.

♥ ♥ ♥

FOODS TO ASK FOR IN RESTAURANTS:

salads with lemon or vinegar *(or bring fat free dressing* packets from home)*

fruit plates or fruit cocktail

tomato juice*

baked potato *(season with fat free dressing* packet brought from home)*

skim milk

steamed vegetables

raw veggies

garbanzo beans*

sliced tomatoes and cucumbers

plain pasta

plain steamed rice

plain breads and rolls *(avoid rich breads like croissants)*

jello

applesauce

fat free desserts such as angel food cake

Marinara sauce* if not made with fat

pasta and steamed vegetables

grilled or roasted vegetables

vegetable shish kabobs

bean soups,* if prepared without fat

*higher sodium food

♥ ♥ ♥

Friends, Families, and Gatherings

Social occasions are challenging, but a few strategies will help you survive. Remind yourself that gatherings are for visiting with others, and learn to "feast" on the conversations. Eating something before will help. Bringing food to a party is a great way to make sure there will be something there for you. Most party givers will appreciate your contribution. Make sure it is one that will fill you up such as a three bean salad. You may find that others will try to sabotage your resolve by getting you to eat a high fat food. This is normal behavior. They might say: "Oh, come on, just once; this won't hurt you," or "You are crazy if you don't try this barbecue. Look, the fat has all dripped away!" Here is an opportunity to show your resolve. It is best to have a rehearsed answer such as:

"I prefer to eat this way."

"My doctor recommended I eat this way because I have heart disease."

"I have three blocked arteries, and I don't want to eat anything that makes them worse."

"Thanks for offering, but I don't want any."

"Just like a diabetic can't eat sugar, I can't eat fat."

♥ ♥ ♥

"See how much fat I can squeeze out of this french fry? (demonstrate) Well, it only takes a pinhead size blockage to clog my artery."

"Hey, people with heart problems end up in the emergency room after holidays and birthdays more than any other time."

Having several alcoholic beverages will lessen your resolve, so make sure you do not overindulge. This can be tough at social occasions. Drink plain water instead—you'll be healthier and happier!

People with heart problems end up in the emergency room after holidays and birthdays more than any other time.

♥ ♥ ♥

Sodium

About thirty percent of heart patients need to be careful about sodium. If you have high blood pressure, congestive heart disease, or a tendency to retain fluids in your tissues, you need to limit your sodium intake to about 2000 milligrams each day. This is equivalent to two grams of sodium. In everyday measurements, 2000 milligrams is about 3/4 of a teaspoon of salt.

Most Americans eat over 6000 milligrams of sodium each day. Everyone would benefit by decreasing salt intake. The government recommends 2400 milligrams each day for all adults.

The taste for salt is an acquired one. We are born with a desire for sweets, but we learn to like salt. Many salty foods reflect our ethnic diversity. Before refrigeration, salt was an important preservative that enabled man to keep and use foods for many months. Because of this, many favorite foods have high levels of salt: spaghetti sauce, pickles, sauerkraut, cheese, salsa, soups, etc.

Sodium is a powerful chemical that attracts water. If you eat a lot of salt, it is processed into your blood, where it draws water. When this happens, your blood volume increases. If you have more blood in your arteries, it causes your blood pressure to increase. Most people eventually pass the excess water through the urine, but some patients do this very slowly. If the excess fluid doesn't leave the body, there is always the danger that it may accumulate in the tissues. Water retention is not a good situation. When retained in the chest cavity, water can lead to congestive heart failure.

Because the taste for salt is acquired, it is possible to "unacquire" a taste for it. If you need to lower your salt intake, read the food labels for sodium and stop eating high sodium foods. Look for reduced sodium products that are also fat free. If you buy canned tomato products, look for cans marked "no added salt". If you use canned beans such as kidney beans, put them in a colander and rinse them well. You will reduce the sodium level about thirty to forty percent. Use more of your favorite herbs and seasoning. Gradually, you will find that the fresh natural taste of food will appeal to you more than the taste of salt. Salty foods may end up tasting "too salty"!

Higher Sodium Foods

pretzels
pickles
sauerkraut
salad dressings
tomato sauce
tomato paste
tomato juice
vegetable juice
canned foods
canned soups and broth
spaghetti sauce
condiments
chips
snack foods
cottage cheese
cheeses

fat free flavored soy meats
dehydrated soups
salsa
onion salt
garlic salt
celery salt
seasoned salt

♥ ♥ ♥

Your Need For Fiber

Fiber helps pull cholesterol out of your body. For that very reason, you need to eat at least 20 to 35 grams of fiber each day. When you follow the **Reversal Food Guide Pyramid** on page 42 and are eating five vegetables each day, along with cooked dried beans, fruits, and whole grain cereals, you will have no problem getting the right amount of fiber. Most patients who use the **Reversal Food Guide Pyramid** on a regular basis have fiber intakes of over 30 grams per day.

As you select foods, pay attention to the fiber content. For example, there is a huge difference between corn flakes and bran flakes when it comes to fiber.  Choose breads that are made of 100% whole wheat flour. Use hot cereals that have the goodness of whole grains, such as Wheatena™ and old fashioned oatmeal.

In addition to lowering cholesterol, fiber also helps to stabilize blood sugar. Many diabetics have found that their blood sugar remains steady when they consistently eat cooked dried beans. Fiber also helps with digestion. It keeps your large intestines healthy because stools are softer and easier to pass. Fiber also helps with weight loss because it fills you up.

Remember, getting enough fiber is not difficult if you follow the **Reversal Food Guide Pyramid** on page 42. Make the effort to eat more of the vegetables that you like along with a host of other good food, and you'll be getting the goodness of fiber in your foods.

♥ ♥ ♥

Caffeine

As you begin to change your lifestyle, you will recognize the value in staying calm and peaceful. Many patients find that caffeine interferes with their path to peace. Some patients are very sensitive to even small amounts of caffeine, such as that found in decaffeinated beverages. Caffeine can interfere with blood pressure and it can cause arterial constriction. It can cause insomnia in some patients and others find it makes them irritable. Some patients find that caffeine causes low blood sugar. Others have found that caffeine contributes to abnormal heart rhythms.

Caffeine is found in coffee, tea (most herbal teas are free of caffeine), chocolate, colas and many types of soda pop, and some medicines such as Anacin™.

♥ ♥ ♥

Dealing With Gas

One common complaint of those starting *The* **"Life Tastes Better Than Steak"** *Eating Plan* is the amount of gas they experience. There are many reasons for this. Vegetarians eat more vegetables and dried beans—foods that promote gas production, especially in the intestine that is not accustomed to these foods. Many people have found that they adjust over time, usually after a few months. Some find they can use strategies to decrease the amount of gas. What seems like a terrible problem during the first six weeks will be less of a problem a year later.

Gas develops from foods made of large molecules. Foods leave the stomach and enter the small intestine in a blended form. Many foods will pass quickly and easily through the intestinal wall into the bloodstream. Foods composed of large molecules, however, are not able to pass through. These foods will wait for enzymes to break them into smaller molecules. If the enzymes are not available or inadequate in volume, the large food molecules have little choice but

to stay in the upper intestine. Foods consisting of large unabsorbed molecules will start to ferment, producing gas. Sometimes the fermentation process is rapid. The large molecules may also draw fluid into the intestine, setting the stage for diarrhea. It is important to know that what causes gas for one person may not bother another person and vice versa. Products like **Beano**™ (1-800-257-8650) and **Lactaid**™ (1-800-522-8243) help prevent gas by breaking up the large molecules. Many people have found these to be important aids in slowing down gas production. There are also products available for gas at your pharmacy. Discuss them with your doctor and pharmacist to determine if they are appropriate for you.

Strategies For Preventing Gas

FOODS   **STRATEGY**

dried beans

♥ always soak dried beans overnight, discard water

♥ always discard cooking liquid

♥ cook beans longer than package recommends

♥ use 1 tsp. dry ginger or 2 tsp. fresh ground ginger in the cooking water for each pound

♥ always rinse canned beans* before using

♥ puree beans in blender after cooking

♥ use **Beano**™ drops or pills before eating beans

♥ try herbs such as fennel or mint

♥ cook each pound with 1/2 tsp. baking soda*

*higher sodium food

♥ ♥ ♥

FOODS	STRATEGY

FOODS

STRATEGY

cabbage family vegetables
and onions

♥ if raw vegetables cause gas,
use cooked until your
digestive system adjusts

♥ use **Beano**™ drops or pills
before eating

milk and other dairy foods

♥ use **Lactaid**™ enzyme

♥ use fat free yogurt and other
cultured fat free foods, often
easier to digest

high fiber foods

♥ use in small quantities,
gradually increasing fiber as
tolerated

♥ gradually introduce whole
grains

raw fruits and vegetables

♥ use applesauce instead of
apples, cooked or canned fruit
instead of raw

♥ puree cooked fruits and
vegetables for easier digestion

♥ gradually increase raw foods

♥ use **Beano**™ drops or pills

higher sodium food

♥ ♥ ♥

Adjusting

The less fat you eat, the less fat you crave. People who "allow" themselves occasionally to indulge in fat have the worst time adjusting. Higher fat foods make you crave more higher fat foods.

People who eat only 10-13 fat grams each day overcome their fat cravings after about 12 weeks. People who continue to eat higher fat foods NEVER lose their fat cravings and *The **"Life Tastes Better Than Steak"** Eating Plan* becomes a difficult, tedious chore.

Give yourself time to let your body adjust. Once you are through the first 12 weeks, it is easier. Give the plan a chance to work by being consistent with 10-13 fat grams each day. Do not deprive yourself of food! Eat frequently throughout the day to nourish yourself and quell hunger. Eat healthy foods and make sure you are getting enough protein.

Skipping Meals:

If you skip breakfast or other meals, you will crave more food late in the afternoon and throughout the evening. If you nourish yourself at breakfast and frequently throughout the day, you will need and want less food at night. People who skip meals tend to eat more calories and often have weight problems. **Do not skip meals.** Care for yourself by providing the fuel your body needs at regular intervals throughout the day. Starvation and deprivation lead to over eating and obesity.

♥ ♥ ♥

Food Needs To Taste Good:

Make sure that you have plenty of good tasting food available. If your food tastes good, you will be happier. As you adjust to The **"Life Tastes Better Than Steak"** Eating Plan, you will change. Textured soy protein may taste weird at first, but after several weeks you will find it tastes good. Keep an open mind about food.

Difficult Times

The most difficult time for sticking to The **"Life Tastes Better Than Steak"** Eating Plan is the first few weeks and months as you are adjusting and learning. Food cravings are very real. For most people following this program, the worst time for cravings has been in the beginning. It takes time for your body to adjust. The less fat you eat, the less fat you will want, but during the first few weeks, your body will put up a fight and you may experience cravings. If you relapse and eat a high fat food, don't wallow in guilt. Just get back on track immediately. Allowing yourself to eat higher fat foods on a regular basis will make you crave more of these foods.

Cravings

One of the most common cravings for women is chocolate. One of the most common cravings for men is meat. Keep track of your cravings. Observe how often you are experiencing cravings and what food you desire. Most people see a decline in their cravings after a few months, but cravings can come back during stressful times. Inadequate protein intake causes cravings for some people, so make sure your meals are balanced and nourishing.

Cravings usually last from three to ten minutes. Find an activity to take your mind off the craving. For example, people who get immersed in hobbies, reading, exercise, or computer activities rarely crave foods while they are busy. On the other hand, people who watch TV report frequent cravings. If a craving lasts longer than ten minutes, you are probably hungry and should eat. If you have a light snack such as juice, fruit, or fat free cookies, your hunger will come back within the hour. Have a substantial snack, such as a bowl of bean soup.

Yoga and meditation are excellent activities to help you deal with cravings. Do your favorite yoga positions and practice deep breathing to quell cravings.

Denial

Another difficult time occurs if you slip into denial about your heart disease. A small number of people have made great progress with the eating plan, only to let it slip away. They felt that they were not as sick "as their doctor said they were." This occurred after progress with cholesterol, weight, or angina.

Denial is a powerful defense mechanism. It makes rational people become irrational. An example is "Jason" (not his real name) who has had two bypass operations and numerous angioplasties. Jason is in his forties and is married. When he started to follow The **"Life Tastes Better Than Steak"** Eating Plan, he was having over 20 angina episodes each week. After six weeks his angina was almost gone and his cholesterol had decreased dramatically. He felt much better and his doctor was extremely pleased. But then something happened to Jason — his thinking became distorted with denial. Because he felt good, he "forgot" about his heart disease. He started to eat foods with fat. Healthy low-fat foods no longer tasted good to him. He began to think that a little bit of this food or that food would not hurt him. Jason's angina started to come back. Fortunately, Jason realized what was happening to him. He coped with his denial and is currently doing very well.

Life Crisis

A third critical period for The **"Life Tastes Better Than Steak"** Eating Plan occurs when you experience a major life crisis. It is a common characteristic for humans to eat more food when under stress. (The exception to this is found in people with anorexia). Don't use a crisis as an excuse; get back on track as soon as you can. Examples of events that may interfere with you food intake:

- death of someone close to you
- sickness, yours or someone close to you
- loss of a job or changes on the job
- retirement, yours or your spouse's
- wedding, yours or someone close to you
- a move to a different house or apartment
- separation or divorce
- difficult relationship with a boss or co-worker
- other events that impact your life

♥ ♥ ♥

Hitting The Wall

It is not uncommon for people to reach a point where lifestyle changes seem to be more of a challenge than they did initially. This usually happens about two or three months after starting the program and it often coincides with a weight loss plateau. It is a common problem and when we talk about it in our support groups, we refer to it as "hitting the wall."

We took this phrase from marathon runners who reach a point when their energy resources are almost gone and they continue running, virtually on determination and instinct. If runners quit the race when they "hit the wall," we would have few people completing marathons. It's the same for heart patients who are working hard making many lifestyle changes. To quit now would be a waste. To quit also means your disease will continue to get worse.

The best thing you can do when you feel like you have hit the wall is to share your feelings with those people who have been supportive of your lifestyle changes. Be open about your feelings of frustration. Ask for help and support. Talking to them and sharing your feelings will help you to cope. If you keep your feelings bottled inside, you are likely to become depressed or angry, and this will make you feel much worse. The people who are closest to you probably recognize how much effort you have put into changing your lifestyle. They may be willing to give you help. Let them know what you have accomplished and that you need their support. If they are not helpful, seek out others who will be.

Your fellow heart patients are the best people to talk to because they are "kindred spirits" who will understand what you are going through. Communicate with those who will help you and avoid those who don't.

It is important to understand that "hitting the wall" is a common experience, one that generally goes away. Many patients have found that meditation, deep breathing, relaxation, and yoga help to deal with it. Do not ignore these vital tools when you are experiencing difficulty with lifestyle changes.

Losing Weight

Cutting back on fat and exercising usually results in weight loss. If weight loss is a goal, you will experience a slow and steady weight loss for several weeks or months. **Keeping a food record is essential.** People who do not keep food records do not succeed as well as those who keep records. The first 10 or 20 pounds you lose are the most important to your heart. Losing weight may cause your metabolism to slow down, even with exercise; and most people find that weight loss diminishes after a few months. This can be frustrating; but if you continue to follow The **"Life Tastes Better Than Steak"** Eating Plan and continue to exercise, your body will continue to get healthier. Progress may be slower. If your weight plateaus and you still want to lose more, examine your habits. Some of the areas that cause difficulty are:

1. SKIPPING MEALS: Skipping meals leads to overeating. People who skip meals eat more food and often weigh more. Eat three meals a day and have some snacks. Nourish yourself on a regular basis.

2. FOOD QUANTITY: Examine your caloric intake. Starvation leads to overeating. People who avoid eating eventually find themselves making up the difference by binge eating, usually with the wrong kind of food. Don't starve yourself. On the other hand, if you are eating large quantities of fat free cookies and other fat free food, you will not lose weight. Be realistic. Too many calories will interfere with weight loss.

3. TIME OF DAY: Examine when you eat. Eating the majority of your foods late in the day will interfere with weight loss. People who eat little food during the day, but heavily in the evening often have weight problems. Eat more at breakfast and at noon. Eat like our grandparents— with a breakfast early in the day, dinner at noon, and a light "supper" in the evening. Mute the TV during commercials so you won't be tempted to go out to the kitchen.

4. LISTEN TO YOUR BODY: Examine your hunger patterns. Listen to your body. Eating breakfast should increase your appetite and help you eat more during the day. Getting into a pattern of eating breakfast will help you eat less food before bed.

5. INADEQUATE PROTEIN INTAKE: Make sure you are getting enough protein. Too many starches may interfere with weight loss.

6. FEELINGS: Examine your feelings. Are you eating to comfort yourself?

Eating to Comfort and Console

Are you an emotional eater who eats because of feelings? Feelings such as boredom, loneliness, relief, or dissatisfaction provide powerful motivation to eat. It is a common trait to use food to comfort and console. As children, many of us were comforted with food and we continue to use food throughout our life.

Emotional eating can lead to obesity and heart disease. The first step to overcome the problem is listening to your body. If you are truly hungry for food, you need to eat. If you are hungry for comfort, then you must give yourself comfort. How do you do this? You need to learn a behavior that provides the comfort your body and mind yearn for. Here are some suggestions:

1. Deep and quiet breathing. Stretch out on the floor on your back. If desired, place a pillow under your knees. Concentrate on calming yourself completely. Take in air deeply through your nose, filling your lungs fully. Push the air out through your mouth by forming a small circle with your lips. Listen to the sound of your breathing and focus on it whenever your mind wanders. Rest and breathe for ten or more minutes. Your urge for food will gradually fade.

2. Sit in a comfortable chair and be still. Close your eyes and communicate a message of help to your higher power. If you have a prayer memorized and prefer to use that, do so. Speak to your God. Express your fears and concerns. Let your higher power know your feelings. Then quietly and patiently listen, while breathing deeply. You may not hear a thing, but continue to listen, every time. Before you finish the session, give thanks to your God for helping you.

3. Share your difficulties with a supportive person. Open your heart and communicate your fears and concerns about your eating problems. For most people, uncontrolled eating is a hidden behavior. By sharing your feelings, you will begin to overcome your eating difficulties.

4. Participate in a support group or in counseling. Both will help give you insight. Feeling connected to others is important in developing the ability to overcome eating problems.

5. Do not hide your feelings from others. The more you hide your feelings, the greater chance you have of using food for comfort. Be open and honest in your communication with others. Let them know your true self, both the good and the bad. When we let others know we are less than perfect, it gives them a chance to be more honest with us. Relationships without pretense are healthier.

Overcoming A Sluggish Metabolism

It is extremely frustrating when weight loss plateaus. Following a healthy eating pattern becomes a chore because your body doesn't seem to be responding. Patients often feel that there is something wrong with them and may express "others can do it, but it won't work for me." The mental image of "something's wrong" is very powerful and can actually interfere with success. Remember, almost all reversal patients go through periods of weight loss plateau. Here are some steps that have helped them:

1. Adjust your attitude. Think positively. Have a winning attitude no matter what. A positive attitude will get your body going in the right direction.

2. Build muscle tissue. Work on simple progressive resistive exercises to build muscle mass. The more muscle you can build, the faster your metabolism will be. You don't need to look like a body builder, but you want your muscles to be firm and strong.

3. Exercise faithfully. "Take" your exercise, like you would an important, life saving medication.

4. Give up sugar. This is a hard one, but it works. Try it for several weeks and you will see and feel a big difference. Sugar is responsible for mood swings, blood glucose fluctuations, high triglycerides, and extra weight. Patients who give it up, love the natural "energy high" that they experience. Remember sugar is in soft drinks, wine coolers, alcohol, lemonade, candy, fat free sweets, fat free ice cream, and even fruit juice.

5. Visualize a thinner you. Visualize your fat cells shrinking. See yourself walking and standing tall, having shed the extra pounds. Do this mental exercise daily: sit comfortably. Relax and close your eyes. Keep your lips closed, but drop your jaw. Drop your shoulders. Relax your neck and upper torso. In this relaxed position, do deep and slow breathing. As you breathe, see in your mind's eye, your fat cells. They are like yellow balloons and you see many in front of you. Now, see the balloons deflating and collapsing. The color gets paler and turns to white. The balloons are small and shriveled, like raisins. See them shrink and gradually disappear. Repeat this over and over. Don't do it once and then think it hasn't worked. Give it a chance to work by doing it daily.

6. Keep a food record every day. Even if your schedule gets totally hectic and out of control, the food record is the most important tool for weight loss.

7. Weigh yourself weekly on the same scale, first thing in the AM. Each month, measure your waist and your hips, seven inches below your waist. Keep these numbers and compare them. You may see little progress on the scale, but the tape measure will change.

♥ ♥ ♥

8. Be with supportive people who will not sabotage or jeopardize your goals. Ignore those who try to interfere with your weight loss. Be strong. To feel strong, do the yoga pose called **Mountain Pose**. This pose is designed to give you stability and confidence. Doing it daily will help you be steady and still, like a mountain.

Cholesterol and Triglycerides

Cholesterol is produced by our livers. When your blood is tested, your total cholesterol represents the cholesterol that is flowing in your blood. Unfortunately, when you have your blood tested there is no way to measure the amount of cholesterol that has built up on your artery walls. People who have total cholesterol over 200 are thought to have more, but this is not always true. Reversal usually occurs when your total cholesterol is 150 or under. An exception is with women taking estrogens. They may not be able to lower cholesterol to levels under 150, but can still experience reversal. Women overall have a more difficult time lowering cholesterol than men.

HDL Cholesterol: This number represents the GOOD cholesterol in your blood—think of the H for "healthy". HDL stands for high density lipoprotein. HDL will not collect on your artery wall, and it plays an important role in removing the bad cholesterol from your body. Because HDL is beneficial, you will want to increase its level; and the best way to do this is through physical exercise. Your HDL should be higher than 35. Most heart patients have low HDL.

When your total cholesterol drops, your HDL usually drops as well. This can be discouraging, but don't let it get you down.

♥ ♥ ♥

Continue to exercise and you will find that your HDL will gradually increase. The increase may only be a few points each year, but this still represents improvement.

LDL Cholesterol: This number represents the BAD cholesterol in your blood—think of the L for "lousy". LDL stands for low-density lipoprotein. LDL collects on your artery wall. LDL production increases with high fat diets and also high calorie diets. When we overeat and don't burn off the calories, the food is converted to fat in our blood (triglycerides). Some of the fat is stored and some may be transformed into LDL cholesterol.

LDL levels should be under 100, but the lower the LDL, the better. You have a better chance of reversing your heart disease when your LDL is under 100.

LDL is especially dangerous because it can oxidize and damage the artery wall. This damage can cause bleeding and clotting that can lead to a heart attack. Most heart patients have high levels of LDL.

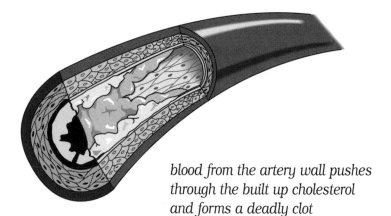

blood from the artery wall pushes through the built up cholesterol and forms a deadly clot

♥ ♥ ♥

Triglycerides: Another important fat is triglyceride. Most of the fats we eat are in the form of triglycerides. If you eat a high fat meal, your blood will soon have lots of triglycerides. In the liver, triglycerides can be (1) processed for the muscles to use as energy, (2) sent to our tummies/hips/thighs etc. to be stored, or (3) processed into LDL cholesterol. When we eat extra calories (even fat free calories), the liver can transform them into triglycerides which can be stored as body fat or eventually processed into LDL. Overweight people tend to have higher triglycerides and weight loss is a treatment for "hypertriglyceridemia" or elevated triglycerides. Concentrated calories from sugar, candy, and alcohol may raise your triglycerides if you are not burning off these extra calories. Some people may be sensitive to the sugar in fruits and fruit juice and use these calories to make triglycerides. And some people have inherited a genetic ability to make a lot of triglycerides.

To lower triglycerides, eat a healthy balance of fruits, vegetables, dried beans, soy products, fat free dairy foods, breads, cereals, and starches. Give up empty calories in foods such as, soda pop, candy, fat free baked goods, juice drinks, and alcoholic beverages. Make sure you take your exercise as faithfully as you take your medications.

A good level for triglycerides is 140 or less. People using *The* **"Life Tastes Better Than Steak"** *Eating Plan* usually experience a slight increase in triglycerides, hovering around 200. As long as you are getting regular exercise and not eating a lot of sweets or alcohol, this increase is not a problem. If your triglycerides are very high (300 or more), weight loss, low-fat eating, and exercise will help to lower them in most cases. Chronically elevated levels may need to be treated with medications. Work with your doctor on a plan that is best for you.

♥ ♥ ♥

Lipid and Weight Guidelines

The two most important numbers to watch are your LDL cholesterol and your weight. Your LDL cholesterol should be under 100 and your weight should be a healthy one for you. Keep tabs on these numbers. If your LDL starts increasing, take action to bring it under 100. Keeping a food record is a powerful tool to lower LDL. You may have to take a cholesterol lowering medication if your LDL remains over 100. Watch your weight. If it starts increasing, take action to stabilize it. Your "ideal" weight is one that makes you feel and look healthy and fit. Focus on becoming leaner and stronger while you decrease body fat. Keep a record of your numbers on this chart:

MY NUMBERS

	Date	Date	Date	Date	Date	Date
Ideal Weight						
LDL Under 100						
Total Cholesterol Under 150						
HDL Over 35						
Triglyceride 140-200						

♥ ♥ ♥

Cholesterol and Stress

One of the most powerful factors leading to the rise of cholesterol is stress. Reversal patients who fail to manage stress have a harder time reversing their disease. Meditation, deep breathing, relaxation and yoga are important tools to learn and practice at least one hour each day. Unfortunately, these techniques are often ignored or glossed over. A heart patient cannot afford to do this.

When you are under stress, your body produces adrenaline. This chemical increases cholesterol production. It is typical for heart patients to have increasing adrenaline levels as the day goes by. The only way to slow adrenaline production is to become quiet and centered through meditation and yoga. When you are in a deep state of relaxation, adrenaline production drops off. This is good news, not only for your cholesterol level, but also for the rest of your body. Adrenaline can increase your blood pressure, constrict your coronary arteries, and increase the clotting factor in your blood. Why risk having high levels of adrenaline released into your body? Suppress adrenaline production daily by using these important and life saving tools.

Sticking to the eating plan and exercising are not sufficient. Meditation, deep breathing, relaxation, and yoga are essential to successful reversal. Use these important tools everyday. In addition, examine your lifestyle. If it is hurried and hectic, find ways to slow it down. Learn to say "no" to activities that will interfere with your path to peace. Instead of forging forth and taking charge, back off and let your life unfold. If you have too much going on, ask for help from supportive people. Think twice

♥ ♥ ♥

before you book yourself into trips and activities that are taxing and where fat free food may not be available.

Your heart problem was your body speaking to you—begging you to slow down and change your lifestyle. If you cannot change the hectic pace of your life, then you can't expect to reverse your blockages.

Reaching Out to Others

As you begin to reap the benefits of The *"Life Tastes Better Than Steak" Eating Plan*, you may want to share your knowledge with others. Some patients get very enthused about the program and spend a lot of time and energy "preaching" to their family and friends. Sometimes, they are disappointed when people don't have a desire to follow the program.

The most successful way to teach others is through example. Let your family and friends watch as you succeed. Then, when they approach you, you can provide them with the tools and knowledge they need. A copy of this eating plan and the cookbook, *"Life Tastes Better Than Steak,"* will get them on the road to success.

♥ ♥ ♥

Resources

The following are helpful resources for recipes and supportive information. Some recipes published by these resources will need to be evaluated for added fat. When oils and other fats are added to the recipes, they no longer meet the criteria.

Dr. Dean Ornish's *Program for Reversing Heart Disease,* Ballantine Books, 1990. Many recipes and great information.

Dr. Dean Ornish's *Eat More, Weigh Less,* Harper Perennial, 1992, and *Everyday Cooking with Dr. Dean Ornish,* Harper Collins, 1996.

The "Life Tastes Better Than Steak" Cookbook, Avery Color Studios and Downriver Cardiology Consultants, 1996. Recipes from patients and staff of a successful heart disease reversal program. 2205 Riverside Drive, Trenton, MI 48183 or P.O. Box 308, Marquette MI 49855. 1-800-722-9925.

Vegetarian Times Magazine, PO Box 446, Mount Morris, IL 61054-8081.Phone 1-800-435-9610. Many recipes and articles that support the vegetarian lifestyle.

Veggie Life Magazine featuring vegetarian recipes. 308 East Hitt St., PO Box 440, Mt. Morris, Illinois 61054-7659.

Fat Free Baking and other books by Sandra Woodruff, RD. Avery Publishing Group, Garden City Park, New York, 1994.

From the Heart, a collection of HeartLife Recipes by Cindy Hughs, RD, and Susan Watson, MS, RD. Heart Institute of Greenville Hospital System, 875 Faris Rd. Greenville, SC 29605. (1-864-455-8890).

Vegetarian Resource Group, VGR, P.O. Box 1463, Baltimore, MD 21203: Information on workshops, foods, recipes. VGR publishes the *Vegetarian Journal* six times/year and offers many publications.

Vegetarian Journal's *Guide to Natural Food Restaurants in the U.S. and Canada.* Avery Publishing Group, Inc. Garden City Park New York:1993.

Simple, Low-fat, and Vegetarian by Suzanne Havala. The Vegetarian Resource Group: 1994.

Cooking Without Fat and *Baking Without Fat* by George Mateljan. Health Valley Foods: 1994

The Almost No-Fat Cookbook by Bryanna Clark Grogan. Order through The Mail Order Catalog, 1-800-695-2241.

500 Fat-Free Recipes by Sarah Schlesinger. Villard Books, New York: 1994.

Healing Heart Foundation. 84-683. Upena Street, Makaha, Hawaii 96792-1935 publishes *Heart Beats* newsletter, the *Healthy Heart Handbook* and e-mail internet support group.

The "Life Tastes Better Than Steak" Eating Plan

♥ ♥ ♥

Your Food Record

TIME	FOOD	Amount	Fat Gm.
DAY ___	DAILY FAT GRAM GOAL _____	DAILY FAT GRAM TOTAL _____	

COPY THIS FOR YOUR PERSONAL USE

♥ ♥ ♥

Your Food Record

TIME	FOOD	Amount	Fat Gm.
DAY ____	DAILY FAT GRAM GOAL _____	DAILY FAT GRAM TOTAL _____	

COPY THIS FOR YOUR PERSONAL USE

♥ ♥ ♥

Fat Gram Counter

Item	Fat Grams	Item	Fat Grams

A

Item	Fat Grams
acerola, 1 c	0.3
adzuki beans, boiled, 1 c	0.2
alcohol	
-beer, 12 oz	0.0
-liquor, 1 oz	0.0
-liqueurs, clear, 1 oz	0.0
-liqueurs, creamy, 1 oz	2.0
-wine, 4 oz	0.0
alfalfa sprouts, 1 c	0.0
almonds, 1 oz.	13.0
almonds, 1/4 c	17.8
anchovies,* 3 items	1.2
amaranth, 1/2 c	0.1
angel food cake,1 pc	0.0
apple 1 med. with skin	0.5
apple 1 med. peeled	0.4
apple crisp (traditional) 1/2 c	13.0
apple juice, 1/2 c	0.2
applesauce, 1/2 c	0.2
apricot, 3 fresh	0.4
apricot, 10 dried halves	0.2
arrowhead, 1 med	0.1
artichoke, 1 med	0.2
artichoke hearts plain, 1/2 c	0.1
artichoke hearts, canned, with oil, 1/2 c	6.8
artificial sweeteners, 1 pkt	0.0
asparagus, 1 c (12 spears)	0.6
au gratin potatoes,* traditional, 1/2 c	9.3
au gratin potatoes*made with skim milk, fat free cheese, no added fat	0.2
au gratin potatoes,* from mix 1/2 c	5.6
avocado, California, 1/4 med	7.5
avocado, Florida, 1/4 med	6.8
avocado dip,* 1/4 c	10.0

B

Item	Fat Grams
Baby Ruth Bar, 2.28 oz	15.0
bacon bits,* 1 tbs	2.0
bacon, Canadian,* 1 oz	2.0
bacon, pork,* 1 slice	3.0
bacon, turkey,* 1 slice	2.5
bacon, Sizzlean,* pork, 1 slice	3.0
bagel, traditional, 1 med	2.0
bagel, frozen, plain, 1 med	1.0
baked potato, plain, 1 med	0.2
baking flour mix,* 1 c	17.0
baking powder,* soda*	0.0
baking mix	
-Bisquik, reg*1 c	17.0
-Bisquik, light*1 c	8.0
bamboo shoots,* 1 c	0.4
banana, fresh, 1 large	0.6
banana, dehydrated, 1 c	1.0
banana chips, fried, 1/4 c	19.0
bar cookies, 2" x 1"	14.0
barbeque sauce,* 3 tbs	1.5
barley, cooked, 1 c	0.7
bass, freshwater, 3.5 oz	2.6
bean dip,* traditional, 1/4 c	10.0
bean dip,* made with no added fat, 1/4 c	0.3
bean salad,* traditional 3 bean, 1/2 c	11.0
bean salad,* canned, 1/2 c	0.3
bean salad,* made with no added fat, 1/2 c	0.5
bean sprouts, mung, 1 c	0.2
bean sprouts, alfalfa, 1 c	0.2
beans, green, 1 c	0.4
beans, fresh, limas, 1 c	0.7
beans, baked and canned*	
-pork and beans*1 c	3.0-4.6
-vegetarian*1 c	1.1

* high in sodium   **If there is fat in the ingredient list, there will be a trace of fat in fat free foods

Item	Fat Grams
beans and peas, dried and then cooked:	
-black beans, 1/2 c	0.4
-blackeye, 1 c	0.9
-chick peas, 1/2 c	2.1
-kidney, 1/2 c	0.4
-lentils, 1 c	0.7
-lima, 1 c	0.7
-navy, 1 c	1.0
-pinto, 1 c	0.9
-red, 1 c	0.9
-split peas, 1 c	0.8
-soybeans, 1 c	15.4
beans, refried*:	
-homemade*1/2 c	13.0
-canned*1/2 c	2.0
-fat free*1/2 c	0.5

BEEF: *the amount listed is for one ounce. Most beef portions are for more than four ounces. To assess the number of grams in a portion, you need to know how much it weighs after cooking. Beef contains saturated fat and will interfere with heart disease reversal.*

Item	Fat Grams
-beef, breaded & fried 1 oz	7.0
-beef brisket, lean, 1 oz	4.0
-beef brisket, untrimmed, 1 oz	9.0
-beef, chipped,* 1 oz	1.0
-beef, chuck, lean, 1 oz	3.0
-beef, chuck, untrimmed, 1 oz	7.0
-beef, corned* brisket, 1 oz	5.0
-beef, corned,* round, 1 oz	4.0
-beef, flank steak, 1 oz	4.0
-beef, ground, 15% fat, 1 oz	4.0
-beef, ground, 20% fat, 1 oz	6.0
-beef, ground, 25% fat, 1 oz	7.0
-beef, ground, 30% fat, 1 oz	7.0
-beef, ground, cooked, rinsed well with very hot water 1 oz	1.0
-beef, ground, Healthy Choice, 1 oz	1.0
-beef, liver, 1 oz	1.0
-beef, ribeye, lean, 1 oz	3.0

Item	Fat Grams
-beef, ribeye, untrimmed, 1 oz	6.0
-beef, rib roast, lean, 1 oz	3.0
-beef, rib roast, prime, 1 oz	6.0
-beef, ribs, prime, 1 oz	12.0
-beef, ribs, lean, 1 oz	6.0
-beef, round, lean, 1 oz	2.0
-beef, round, untrimmed, 1 oz	4.0
-beef, sirloin tip, lean, 1 oz	2.0
-beef, sirloin tip, untrimmed, 1 oz	4.0
-beef, tenderloin, lean, 1 oz	2.0
-beef, tenderloin, prime, 1 oz	4.0
-beef, sirloin, lean, 1 oz	3.0
-beef, sirloin, prime, 1 oz	6.0
-beef, Porterhouse, lean, 1 oz	3.0
-beef, Porterhouse, prime, 1 oz	6.0
-beef, T Bone, lean, 1 oz	3.0
-beef, T Bone, prime, 1 oz	8.0
-beef, stew meat, lean, 1 oz	3.0
-beef, stew meat, trimmed, 1 oz	7.0
-beef stew with gravy and vegetables*:	
-meat trimmed 1 c	8.0
-meat untrimmed 1 c	18.0
beef stroganoff, traditional, 1 c	16.4
beer, 12 oz	0.0
beets, fresh, 1 c	0.2
beet tops, 1 c	0.2
Big Mac,* 1 item	26.0
Bisquik,* 1 c	17.0
Bisquik light,* 1 c	8.0
biscuit,* refrigerated: rely on label	
most brands, 1 item	5.0-11.0
Pillsbury, plain,* 1 item	1.0
biscuit,* 5", homemade, 1	5.8
biscuit,* from mix, 1 item	3.3
black beans, cooked, 1/2 c	0.4
black turtle beans ,1 c	0.6
blackberries, 1 c	0.6
blackeye peas, 1c	0.9
blueberries, 1 c	0.6

* high in sodium   **If there is fat in the ingredient list, there will be a trace of fat in fat free foods

The "Life Tastes Better Than Steak" Eating Plan

♥ ♥ ♥

Item	Fat Grams
bluefish, 3.5 oz	3.3
bologna,* traditional ,1 oz	8-12.0
bouillon,* 1 c	0.5
boysenberries, 1/2 c	0.2
bran, oat, 1 c	2.0
bran, wheat, 1 tbs	0.0
bran, corn, 1 c	0.7
bratwurst, 3 oz	24.0
Braunschweiger,* 1 oz	9.0
bread, bun, 1 bun	2.0
bread crumbs, 1 c	4.6
bread flour, 1 c	3.0
bread, roll, 1 roll	2.0
bread stick, 5," 1 oz	1.0
bread stuffing,* traditional, 1/2 c	14.0
bread stuffing,* mix, 1/2 c	8.7
bread, white or wheat, 1 slice	1.0
brewer's yeast, 1 oz	1.4
broad beans, 1 c	0.6
broccoli, 1 c	0.2
broth,* strained, 1 c	0.5
brown rice, 1 c	1.8
brownie, 1' x 2", 1 item	4.0-17.0
Brussels sprouts, 1 c (eight sprouts)	0.8
buckwheat groats, 1 c	1.2
buckwheat flour, dark, 1c	2.5
buckwheat flour, light, 1 c	1.2
bulgur, dry, 1 c	1.9
bun, hamburger, 1 bun	2.0
bun, hotdog, 1 bun	2.0
burdock, 1 c	0.2
burrito,* fast food:	
beef,* 1	19.0
bean,* 1	11.0
burrito shell, 1 item	2.0
burrito shell, fat free**	trace
butter, 1 tsp	3.8
butterbeans, 1 /2 c	0.8

Item	Fat Grams
buttermilk*:	
skim,* 1 c	0.4
cultured,* 1 c	2.2
butterscotch topping, 1 tbs	1.0

C

Item	Fat Grams
cabbage, 1 c	0.2
cabbage, Chinese, 1 c	0.2
cabbage roll*	
-beef and rice,* 1 roll	7.0
-beef, no rice,* 1 roll	19.0
Caesar salad,* 1 c	8.0
cafe au lait, 1 c	3.0
cake*:	
-unfrosted,* 1 med. piece	10.2
-frosted,* 1 med. piece	15.0
Canadian bacon,* 1 oz	2.0
candy:	
-hard, jelly, gummy, 1 piece	0.0
-solid chocolate, 1 oz	9.0
-chocolate and nuts, 1 oz	10.0
-marshmallow, 1 oz	0.0
-mints, plain, 1 item	0.0
-M & M's, plain, 1.7 oz	10.0
-M & M's, peanut, 1.7 oz	12.0
candy bars: (use label)	
-Baby Ruth, 2.28 oz	15.0
-granola bar, 1 med	5.0
-Krackel, 1.45 oz	12.0
-milk chocolate, 1 oz	9.0
-with nuts, 1 oz	10.0
-Milky Way, 2.1 oz	8.0
-Mr. Goodbar, 1.65 oz	17.0
-Payday, 1.8 oz	14.0
-Peanutbutter Cups, 1.6 oz	15.0
-Snickers, 2 oz	13.0
-3 Musketeers, 2.1 oz	8.0
canola oil, 1 tbs	14.0
cantaloupe, 1 c	0.5
cappuccino, 3/4 c	2.1

* high in sodium   **If there is fat in the ingredient list, there will be a trace of fat in fat free foods

Item	Fat Grams
carob candy, 1 oz	2.0
carob flour, 1 c	3.7
carp, 3.5 oz	5.8
carrot, 1 c	0.1
carrot, 1 medium	0.1
carrot juice, 3/4 c	0.3
caramel topping, 1 tbs	1.0
caramels, 3	2.0
casaba melon, 1 c	0.2
cashews,* 1/4 c	15.9
catfish, 3.5 oz	3.1
cauliflower, 1 c	0.2
catsup,* 1 tbs	0.1
caviar,* 1 tbs	2.9
celery, 1 c	0.2
celery, one stalk, 7.5 inches long	0.1
cereal, cold—ready to eat: rely on label	
-wheat based, 1 c	1.0
-rice based, 1 c	0.0
-corn based, 1 c	0.1
-oat based, 1 c (varies)	4.0
-with nuts, seeds, 1/4 c	5.0
-wheat germ, 1/4 c	4.0
cereal, hot:	
-cream of rice, 3/4 c	0.1
-cream of wheat, 1 c	0.5
-grits, 3/4 c	0.5
-oat bran, 1 c	2.5
-oatmeal, 1 c	1.9
chard, Swiss, 1 c	0.2
cheese, cottage*	
-whole,* 1 c	10.2
-2%,* 1 c	4.4
-low-fat 1%,* 1 c	2.3
-fat free,* 1 c	trace
cheese, cream*	
-regular,* 1 oz	9.5
-low-fat, 2%* 1 oz	4.7
-fat free,* 1 oz	trace

Item	Fat Grams
cheese, cheddar:*	
-regular,* 1 oz	9.0
-lowfat,* 1 oz	5.0
-fat free,* 1 oz	trace
cheese, imitation* (cheese food)	
-regular,* 3/4 oz	9.0
-lowfat,* 3/4 oz	5.0
-light,* 3/4 oz	2.0
-fat free,* 3/4 oz	trace
cheese* mozzarella	
-regular,* 1 oz	7.0
-part skim,* 1 oz	4.5
-fat free,* 1 oz	trace
cheese, parmesan*	
-regular,* 1 tbs	1.9
-regular,* 1 ounce	7.3
-lowfat,* 1 tbs	1.0
-fat free,* 1 tbs	trace
cheese, ricotta	
-regular, 1/2 c	16.0
-part skim, 1/2 c	10.0
-fat free, 1 oz	trace
cheese, roquefort,* 1 oz	8.7
cheese, spread,* 1 tbs	5.7
cheese puffs,* 1 c (30)	12.0
cheese sauce,* 2 oz	4.1
cheese Swiss*	
-regular,* 1 oz	7.8
-processed,* 1 oz	7.1
-lowfat,* 1 oz	3.0
-fat free,* 1oz	trace
cheese soup*	
-whole milk,* 1 c	15.0
-skim milk,* 1 c	11.0
cheeseburger,* fast food	13.0
cheesecake,* 9' diameter, made with:	
-cottage cheese,* 1/8th pie	12.0
-cream cheese,* 1/8th pie	38.0
cherries, 10 cherries	0.7
chestnuts,* waterpacked, 1 c	0.2

* high in sodium   **If there is fat in the ingredient list, there will be a trace of fat in fat free foods

The "Life Tastes Better Than Steak" Eating Plan

♥ ♥ ♥

Item	Fat Grams
chickpeas, garbanzos, 1/2 c	2.1
CHICKEN: *The amounts given are for one ounce. Most portions are three to eight ounces.*	
-skinless, white, 1 oz	1.0
-skinless, dark, 1 oz	2.0
-with skin, white, 1 oz	3.0
-with skin, dark, 1 oz	4.0
chicken, Cornish hen	
-white, with skin 1 oz	3.0
-dark, with skin 1 oz	4.0
chicken, fried in batter with skin	
-breast, 1	25.0
-leg, 1	16.0
-thigh, 1	19.0
-wing, 1	19.0
chicken hotdog,* 1 frank	11.0
chicken giblets, 1 oz	1.0
chicken pot pie,* 1 item	24.0
chicken roll,* 1 oz	2.0
chicken salad*	
-with mayonnaise, 1/2 c 18-22.0	
-with salad dressing, 1/2 c	17.0
-with fat free dressing, 1/2 c 6.0-8.0	
chicken sandwich, fast food*:	
-Arby's, 1 item	22.5
-BK broiler, 1 item, plain	8.0
-McD, 1 item	20.0
chicken stew,* 1 c	6.0
chicken fried steak, 1 oz	7.0
chicory greens, raw, 1 c	0.6
chili, no beans,* 1 c	19.0
chili, meat and beans,* 1 c	15.0
chili, no meat,* no added fat, 1 c	1.0
chili dog,* fast food, 1	20.0
chili sauce,* 1 tbs	1.0
chipped beef,* 1 oz	1.0
chipped beef,* creamed, 1 c	20.0

Item	Fat Grams
chips: *grams vary; rely on label*	
-corn,* 15 chips	8.0
-potato,* 13 chips	10.0
-potato,* rippled, 10 chips	11.9
-potato,* sour cream, 10 chips	13.0
-tortilla* 10 chips	5.0
-Baked Tostitos™, 1 oz	1.0
chives, 1 tbs	0.0
chocolate, bittersweet, solid, 1 oz	11.3
chocolate candy, 1 oz	8.9
chocolate candy, with nuts, 1 oz	10.8
chocolate chips, 1 oz	10.2
chocolate, cocoa powder, 1/3 c	2.8
chocolate, cocoa powder, 1 tbs	1.5
chocolate flavor mix, 3 tbs	0.7
chocolate milk, whole, 1 c	8.3
chocolate milk, 2%, 1 c	5.0
chocolate milk, skim, 1 c	0.5
chocolate, semi-sweet chunks or bits, 1 oz	10.2
chocolate syrup, 2 tbs	0.3
chow mein,* meatless, 1 c	7.0
chow mein,* with meat, 1 c	11.0
chow mein noodles,* 1 c	11.0
chowder, clam*	
-Manhattan,* 1 c	2.9
-New England,* 1 c, traditional recipe	6.0
-New England,* 1 c, with cream	36.0
-New England,* 1 c, made w/skim milk .	3.4
cinnamon, 1 tsp	0.0
cinnamon bread, 1 slice	1.0
cinnamon roll, 1	14.0
clams, 5 large	0.9
clam, chowder*	
-Manhattan,* 1 c	2.9
-New England,* reg., 1c	6.0
-New England,* 1 c, made w/skim milk .	3.4
clam juice,* 1 c	0.2
cocktail sauce,* 1 tbs	0.0
cocoa, hot, whole milk, 1 c	10.0

* high in sodium   **If there is fat in the ingredient list, there will be a trace of fat in fat free foods

Item	Fat Grams	Item	Fat Grams
cocoa, hot, skim milk, 1 c	2.0	-peanut butter, 1 item	3.0
cocoa powder, 1/3 c	2.8	-sugar cookie, 1 item	1.4
cocoa powder, 1 tbs	0.5	-vanilla wafer, 1 item	1.6
coconut milk, 1 c	57.2	-vanilla sandwich. 1 item	2.0
coconut, shredded, 1 tbs	1.7	cordials, 2 oz	0.0
cod fish, 3.5 oz	0.3	corn	
coffee, 1 c	0.0	-canned,* creamed, 1 c	1.0
coffee, cappuccino, 6 oz	2.1	-canned,*or frozen, 1 c	2.2
coffee, flavored, rely on label		-fresh, 1 ear	0.9
coffee cake,* 3"x3"x1", 1 piece	10.0	corn bread,* 3" x 3" x1", 1 piece	8.0
coldcuts* (rely on label when possible)		corn chips* 15 chips	8.0
-Braunschweiger,* 1 oz	9.0	corn dog,* 1 item	20.0
-bologna,* 1 oz	7.0	corn flour, 1 c	3.0
-ham,* lean, 1 oz	2.0	corn grits, 1 c	0.5
-turkey ham,* 1 oz	2.0	corn meal	
-pressed meat,* 1 oz	1.0	-degerminated, 1 c	1.7
-salami,* cooked, 1 oz	6.0	-whole grain, 1 c	4.8
-salami,* hard, 1oz	10.0	corn oil, 1 tbs	14.0
-spam,* 1 oz	9.0	corn syrup, 1 tbs	0.0
coleslaw *		corned beef, *round, 1 oz	5.0
-with mayo,* 1/2 c	15.0	corned beef,* brisket, 1 oz	4.0
-with salad dressing,* 1/2 c	9.0	cornstarch, 1 tbs	0.0
-with non-fat mayo,* 1/2 c	0.0	cottage cheese:*	
-with clear dressing,* 1/2 c	9.0	-fat free,* 1 c	trace
-with fat free dressing,* 1/2 c	0.1	-lowfat, 1%,* 1 c	2.3
collards, boiled, 1 c	0.8	-lowfat, 2%,* 1 c	4.4
condensed milk,* 1 c	26.6	-regular, 4%,* 1 c	10.2
cone, no ice cream, 1 plain	0.7	cottonseed oil, 1 tbs	14.0
cone with soft serve	12.0	cowpeas, 1c	0.9
cone with ice cream		crab, canned,* 1/2 c	2.1
-1 c regular	7.0	crab, fresh, 3.5 oz	1.5
-1 c high fat	12.0	cracked wheat bread, 1 slice	0.9
-1 c ice milk	4.0	crackers:	
cookies: (use label when available)		-cheese,* 5 pieces	4.9
-brownies, 2" x 1", 1 item	4.0-17.0	-graham, 2 squares	2.0
-chocolate chip, 1 item	3.0-7.0	-melba, 4 crackers	0.0
-fig bars, 1 item	1.0	-matzo, 6" round, 3 crackers	1.0
-fortune cookie, 1 item	1.0	-oyster crackers,* 10 items	1.0
-oatmeal, 1 item	2.6	-Ritz, *4 crackers	3.0
-Oreo, 1 item	2.0	-soda, saltine,* 3 squares	1.0

* high in sodium   **If there is fat in the ingredient list, there will be a trace of fat in fat free foods

♥ ♥ ♥

Item	Fat Grams
crackers, continued	
-Zwieback, 2 pieces	1.0
-Wheat Thins,* 8 crackers	3.0
cranberries, 1 c	0.2
cranberry beans, 1 c, boiled	0.8
cranberry juice cocktail, 1 c	0.1
cream:	
-fat free creamer, most brands, 1 tsp	0.4
-creamer, non-dairy, 1 tsp	2.0
-creamer, non-dairy, 1 tbs	6.0
-half and half, 1 tsp	0.6
-half and half, 1 tbs	1.7
-heavy cream, 1 tbs	5.6
-sour cream, reg., 1 tbs	2.5
-sour cream, skim, 1 tbs	trace
-whipped topping, 1 tbs	1.0
-whipped cream, 1 tbs	3.0
-heavy whipping cream, 1 tbs	5.6
cream cheese:	
-cream cheese,* regular, 1 tbs	9.5
-cream cheese,* part skim, 1 oz	4.7
-cream cheese,* fat free, 1 oz	trace
cream of wheat, 1 c, cooked	0.5
cream puff, filled, 1 puff	18.1
cream of rice cereal, 3/4 c	0.1
creamer, non-dairy, 1 tsp	1.0
crepe, 6," 1 item	1.0
croissant, 5", 1 item	13.0
croutons* 1/4 c	2.0
cucumber, 1/2 c, sliced	0.1
cucumber, 1 whole	0.6
cup cake,* plain, 1 item	4.0
cup cake,* frosted, 1 item	5.5
currants, raw, 1 c	0.2
currants, dried, 1 c	0.2
custard, 1/2 c	7.0

D

Item	Fat Grams
dandelion greens, raw, 1/2 c chopped	0.3
Danish pastry, 3" x 3", 1 item	13.8

Item	Fat Grams
dates, 1 item	0.0
dates, diced, 1c	0.8
deviled eggs*	
-regular recipe,* 1/2 egg	5.0
-no yolks & fat free mayo,* 1/2 white	0.0
dip*:	
-bean,* 1/4 c	1.0
-cottage cheese,* 1/4 c	1.0
-guacamole,* 1/4 c	10.0
-sour cream,* 1/4 c	10.0
-yogurt based,* 1/4 c	1.0
divinity, 1 piece	0.0
doughnut,* 3" cake, 1	17.0
doughnut, 4" raised, 1	10.0
dressing,* bread, 1/2 c	14.0
dressing,* salad: rely on product label**	
-miracle whip, 1 tbs	7.0
-miracle whip, lowfat, 1 tbs	5.0
-miracle whip, fat free, 1 tbs	0.0
-clear dressing, regular, 1 tbs	7.0
-creamy dressing, 1 tbs	6.0
-fat free, 1 tbs	trace**
drinks, mixed	
-clear, no cream, 2 oz	0.0
-Irish Coffee, 2 oz	4.0
-pina colada, 2 oz	4.0
-grasshopper, 2 oz	4.0
duck, with skin, 1 oz	7.0
duck, without skin, 1 oz	3.0
dumpling,* 2", 1 item	4.0

E

Item	Fat Grams
eclair, 1 item	12.0
egg, 1 whole large	5.6
egg, boiled, 1 whole large	5.6
egg, poached, 1 whole large	5.6
Egg Beaters,™ 1 c	0.0
egg foo yung,* 1 piece	17.0
egg McMuffin,* 1	11.2
egg noodles, 1 c	2.4

* high in sodium   **If there is fat in the ingredient list, there will be a trace of fat in fat free foods

Item	Fat Grams
egg salad*:	
-with mayonnaise, 1/2 c	22.0
-with miracle whip, 1/2 c	17.0
-with egg white, non-fat mayo, 1/2 c	0.0
egg substitutes:	
-Egg Beaters, 1/2 c	0.0
-Scramblers, fat free, 1/2 c	0.0
-2nd Nature, fat free, 1/2 c	0.0
-with cheese	6.0
egg, deviled,* 1/2	5.0
egg, scrambled or fried:	
-cooked with fat, 2 large	19.0
-cooked without fat, 2 large	11.2
egg, whites only, 2 large	0.0
eggnog, 1 c	15.0
eggplant, plain, 1 c	0.2
eggplant, breaded and fried, 3 slices	45.0
eggroll* 1 item	7.0
enchiladas,* beef, 1 item	14.0
enchiladas,* cheese, 1 item	17.0
enchiladas,* chicken, 1 item	9.0
endive, 1/2 c chopped	0.1
English muffin, 1	1.0
Eskimo pie, 1 item	13.0
evaporated milk,* skim, 1 c	0.6
evaporated milk,* whole, 1 c	19.0

F

Item	Fat Grams
falafel,* 1 patty	7.0
farina, 1 c dry	1.6
farina, cooked, 3/4 c	0.2
farmer cheese,* whole, 1 oz	7.0
farmer cheese,* low-fat, 1 oz	2.0
fava beans,* canned, 8 oz	0.6
feta cheese,* 1 oz	6.0-9.0
fettuccini Alfredo,* 1 c	28.0
figs, fresh, 1 large	0.2
figs, dried, 10 large	0.2

Item	Fat Grams
FISH:	

- *All portions listed are cooked with no added fat, unless otherwise noted..*
- *Basting or broiling fish with fat or oil will add 2 grams of fat per ounce.*
- *A ten ounce broiled dinner portion cooked or basted with oil: add 20 fat grams to the fish's fat grams.*
- *Breading and frying will add 5 grams of fat per ounce.*
- *A ten ounce dinner portion lightly breaded and sauteed in oil:add 50 fat grams to the fish's fat grams! When doctors tell heart patients to eat more fish, the worst thing a patient can do is eat fish basted or fried in oil, butter, or any kind of fat.*
- *Most of the portions listed here are for 3.5 ounces, which is about 4 inches long and three inches wide and about 3/4 inch thick.*
- *Most luncheon portions of fish in restaurants are about 3.5 ounces.*
- *Most dinner portions of fish in restaurants will be about 8 to 10 ounces. To convert the fat grams in 3.5 ounces to the fat grams found in 10 ounces: multiply the fat grams by 2.9.*

Item	Fat Grams
-fish, abalone, 3.5 oz	0.3
-fish, anchovy, 3 items	1.2
-fish, anchovy paste, 1 teaspoon	0.8
-fish, bass, freshwater, 3.5 oz	2.6
-fish, bass, black, 3.5 oz	1.2
-fish, bass, saltwater, striped, 3.5 oz	2.7
-fish, bluefish, 3.5 oz	3.3
-fish, buffalo fish, 3.5 oz	4.2
-fish, butterfish, gulf, 3.5 oz	2.9
-fish, butterfish, northern, 3.5	10.2
-fish, cakes, frozen and fried, 3.5 oz	14.0
-fish, carp, 3.5 oz	5.8
-fish catfish, 3.5 oz	3.1
-fish, caviar, 1 tbs	4.5
-fish, clams, canned, drained, 3 oz	2.5
-fish, clams fresh, 5 large	0.9
-fish, cod, 3.5 oz	0.3

* high in sodium   **If there is fat in the ingredient list, there will be a trace of fat in fat free foods

The "Life Tastes Better Than Steak" Eating Plan

♥ ♥ ♥

Item	Fat Grams
fish, continued:	
-fish, crab, canned, 1/2 c	2.1
-fish, crab, fresh Alaskan, 3.5 oz	1.5
-fish, crab cake, 3.5 oz	10.8
-fish, crappie, white, 3.5 oz	0.8
-fish, croaker, Atlantic, 3.5 oz	3.2
-fish, croaker, white, 3.5 oz	0.8
-fish, cusk ,3.5 oz	0.7
-fish, dolphin, 3.5 oz	0.7
-fish, eel, American, 3.5 oz	18.3
-fish, eulachon	2.1
-fish fillets, frozen, battered, 3 oz	10.0
-fish, flatfish, 3.5 oz	0.8
-fish, flounder, 3.5 oz	0.5
-fish, gefilte fish, 3.5 oz	2.2
-fish, grouper, 3.5 oz	1.3
-fish, haddock, 3.5 oz	0.6
-fish, halibut, 3.5 oz	1.2
-fish, herring, 3.5 oz	11.3
-fish, herring, canned/smoked 3.5 oz	13.6
-fish, herring, pickled, 3.5 oz	15.1
-fish, Jack mackerel, 3.5 oz	5.6
-fish, kingfish, 3.5 oz	3.0
-fish, lake trout, 3.5 oz	6.5
-fish, lobster, 3.5 oz	1.9
-fish, mackerel, Atlantic, 3.5 oz	12.2
-fish, mackerel, Pacific, 3.5 oz	7.3
-fish, mahimahi, 3.5 oz	1.2
-fish, monk, 3.5 oz	1.2
-fish, muskellunge, 3.5 oz	2.5
-fish, mussels, 3.5 oz	2.2
-fish, ocean perch, 3.5 oz	1.2
-fish, octopus, 3.5 oz	0.8
-fish, orange roughy, 3.5 oz	7.0
-fish, oysters, 5 to 8 medium items	1.8
-fish, oysters, canned, 3.5 oz	2.2
-fish, perch, freshwater, 3.5 oz	0.9
-fish, perch, ocean, 3.5 oz	1.2
-fish, pickerel 3.5 oz	0.5
-fish, pike, blue, 3.5 oz	0.9
-fish, pike, northern, 3.5 oz	1.1

Item	Fat Grams
-fish, pike, walleye, 3.5 oz	1.2
-fish, pollock, 3.5 oz	1.0
-fish, pompano, 3.5 oz	9.5
-fish, red snapper, 3.5	1.9
-fish, rockfish, 3.5 oz	2.5
-fish, roughy, orange 3.5	7.0
-fish, salmon, Atlantic, 3.5 oz	6.3
-fish, salmon, chinook, 3.5 oz	14.0
-fish, salmon,* pink, canned, 3.5 oz	5.1
-fish, salmon,* red, canned, 3.5 oz	3.7
-fish, salmon,*smoked, 3.5 oz	9.3
-fish, salmon, sockeye, 3.5 oz	8.5
-fish, salmon, skinless, ocean, 3.5 oz	3.5
-fish sandwich,* fast food, 1 item	27.0
-fish, sardines,* in oil, 2 items	2.8
-fish, scallops, 3.5 oz	1.2
-fish, sea bass, 3.5 oz	1.5
-fish, shrimp, 3.5 oz	1.8
-fish, smelt, 3.5 oz	2.1
-fish, smelt, canned, 4-5 items	13.5
-fish, sole, 3.5 oz	0.5
-fish, squid, 3.5 oz	1.2
-fish sticks, baked, 3.5 oz	10.5
-fish, sushi, 3.5 oz	4.9
-fish, swordfish, 3.5 oz	4.0
-fish, trout, brook, 3.5 oz	2.1
-fish, trout lake, 3.5 oz	6.5
-fish, trout, rainbow, 3.5 oz	1.2
-fish, tuna,* canned, *read label because there can be a wide range of fat grams, depending on the type of tuna. Water packed tuna is not always low in fat grams*	
-fish, tuna,* canned light, in oil, 3.5 oz	8.1
-fish, tuna,* canned light, in water, 3.5 oz	2.4
-fish, tuna,* canned, white, in oil, 3.5 oz	8.0
-fish, tuna,* canned, white, in water, 3.5 oz	2.4
-fish, tuna, fresh albacore, 3.5 oz	7.5

* high in sodium   **If there is fat in the ingredient list, there will be a trace of fat in fat free foods

Item	Fat Grams
fish, continued:	
-fish, tuna, fresh bluefin, 3.5 oz	4.1
-fish, tuna, fresh yellowfin, 3.5 oz	3.0
-fish, white perch, 3.5 oz	3.9
-fish, whitefish, 3.5 oz	5.8
-fish, whiting, 3.5 oz	1.7
-fish, yellowtail, 3.5 oz	5.4
flour, white, 1 c	1.0
flour, wholewheat ,1 c	0.5
frankfurters*: rely on product label	
-frankfurters, poultry,* 1 item	8.0-13.0
-frankfurters, beef or pork,* 1 item	13.0
-frankfurters, fat free* emulsion product, 1 item**	0.0-0.4
-frankfurters, Healthy Choice,* 1 item	2.0
-frankfurters, Hormel,* low-fat, 1 item	1.0
French beans, 1 c	1.3
French bread, 1 slice	1.1
French fries,*	
-fast food, small serving*	10.0
-fast food, large serving*	22.0
-restaurant, 1 c*	6.0
-homemade, 1 c*	4.9
French toast, regular, 1 slice	11.0
French toast made with egg white and vegetable oil cooking spray, 1 slice	2.0
frosting, regular, 1 tbs	2.0
frosting, 7 minute,1 tbs	0.0
frozen yogurt, read label, products vary	
fruit bread,* 4.5x2.5x.5", 1 slice	3.0
fruit bread* with nuts, 1 slice	8.0
fruit cocktail, 1 c	1.1
fruit crisp, traditional, 1/2 c	13.0
fruit flavored drinks, 1 c	0.0
fruit pie, 1/8th, 1 piece	13.0
fruit pie tart, Hostess,1 item	23.0
fruit relish, 1 tbs	0.0
fruit roll-ups, 1 item	0.1
fruit salad, no dressing, 1 c	0.1
fruit sauce, 1 tbs	0.0
fudgies, 1 piece	1.0
fudge topping, 1 tbs	3.0-5.0

Item	Fat Grams
G	
garbanzo beans, fresh, boiled 1/2 c	2.1
garbanzo beans, canned,* 1/2 c	1.4
garlic, 1 clove	0.3
gefilte fish,* 3x2x1", 1 piece	2.2
gelatin, unflavored, 1 pkt	0.0
gelatin dessert, 1 c	0.0
giblets, 1 oz	1.3
gimlet, 2 oz	0.0
ginger root, 1/4 c	0.2
goose with skin, 1 oz	7.0
goose, skinless, 1 oz	3.0
gooseberries, 1 c	0.9
graham cracker crust, 1/8 pie	5.0-8.0
graham crackers, 2 squares	2.0
granola, 1/4 c	0.5
granola bar, 1 item	5.0
grapes, 1 c	0.3
grape juice, 1 c	0.0
grapefruit, 1 whole	0.2
grapefruit juice, 1 c	0.0
gravy,* traditional, 1/4 c	5.0
green pepper, sweet, 1/2 c chopped	0.1
green pepper, stuffed,* traditional recipe, 1 item	15.0
green pepper, stuffed, meatless- no added fat, 1 item	1.0
grenadine, 1 tbs	<1.0
grits, 1 c	0.5
ground beef casserole,* 1 c	19.0
ground beef, four ounce pattie	
-15% fat, 4 oz	19.3
-20% fat, 4 oz	23.4
-25-30% fat, 4 oz	30.0
-ground beef cooked and washed in very hot water, 1 oz	1.0
ground turkey, four ounce pattie	
-meat and skin 4 oz	16.0
-white meat only 4 oz	4.0
-ground turkey cooked and washed in very hot water 1 oz	1.0
guacamole dip,* 1/4 c	10.0

* high in sodium   **If there is fat in the ingredient list, there will be a trace of fat in fat free foods

The "Life Tastes Better Than Steak" Eating Plan

Item	Fat Grams
H	
haddock, 3.5 oz	0.6
half and half, 1 tsp	0.6
half and half, 1 tbs	1.7
halibut, 3.5 oz	1.2
ham,* cured, (traditional, pork)	
-regular ham,* 1 oz	4.0
-lean,* 1 oz	3.0
-boiled,* 1 oz	3.0
-deviled, canned,* 1 oz. (2 tbs.)	6.0
ham and cheese* fast food sandwich* 1 item	16.0
ham salad,* 1/2 c	36.3
hamburger, fast food:	
-small, plain, 1 item	11.1
-cheeseburger,* 1 item	13.8
-1/4 pounder, 1 item	20.7
-1/4 pounder with cheese,* 1 item	28.0
-Big Mac,* 1 item	26.0
-Whopper,* 1 item	36.0
-Whopper & cheese,* 1 item	44.0
hamburger meat	
-Healthy Choice, 4 oz	4.0
-15% fat, 4 oz	19.3
-20% fat, 4 oz	23.4
-30% fat, 4 oz	30.0
-hamburger meat, cooked and rinsed well with very hot water, 4 oz	4.0
hash, beef,* 1 c	31.0
hash brown potatoes, 1/2 c	10.9
herring, fresh, 3.5 oz	11.3
Hi C, 1 c	0.0
hollandaise sauce,* 1 tbs	7.0
hominy, canned,* white, 1 c	0.7
hominy, canned,* yellow, 1 c	0.6
hominy grits, 1 c	0.5
honey, 1 tbs	0.0
honeydew, 1c	0.2
horseradish, 1 tbs	0.0

Item	Fat Grams
hotdogs: rely on product label	
-hotdog, no bun,* 1 item	13.0
-hotdog, chicken,* 1 item	8.0-13.0
-hotdog, turkey,* 1 item	8.0-13.0
-hotdog, Healthy Choice, regular,* 1 item	1.0
-hotdog, Healthy Choice, jumbo,* 1 item	2.0
-hotdog, fat free emulsion meat product,* 1 item**	0.1-0.4
-hotdog, Hormel low-fat* 1 item	1.0
-hotdog on bun* fast food* 1 item	19.0
-hotdog on bun, home cooked* 1 item	15.0
hotdog bun, 1 bun	2.0
hushpuppy,* 1 item	12.0
I	
ice cream, read label	
-premium, 1/2 c	12.0
-regular, 1/2 c	7.0
-ice milk, 1/2 c	2.0
-frozen yogurt, 1/2 c	2.0
-fat free, 1/2 c	trace
-frozen tofu, 1/2 c	12.0
ice cream bar, traditional, 1 item	13.0
ice cream cone, no ice cream	0.7
ice cream topping, always read label	
-caramel or butterscotch syrup, 3 tbs	3.0
-fudge sauce, 1 tbs	2.8
-chocolate syrup, 2 tbs	0.3
-pineapple topping, 3 tbs	0.2
-strawberry sauce, 3 tbs	0.1
ice milk, 1/2 c	2.0
icing, regular, 1 tbs	2.0
icing, 7 minute,1 tbs	0.0
Irish Cream, 2 oz	4.0
Italian bread, 1 slice	0.6
Italian ice, 1/2 c	0.0
Italian sausage,* 3 oz	22.0

* high in sodium   **If there is fat in the ingredient list, there will be a trace of fat in fat free foods

Item	Fat Grams
J	
jam, all fruit jam, 1 tbs	<0.1
jello, 1 c	0.0
jelly, 1 tbs	0.0
jelly beans, 1 item	0.0
Jerusalem artichoke, 1 c	0.0
juice, fruit 1 c varies from .1 to .5, see specific juices	
juice, vegetable* 1 c varies from .1 to .3, see specific juices	
K	
kale, 1c	0.6
kasha, cooked, 1 c	1.2
ketchup,* 1 tbs	0.1
kidney beans, 1/2 c	0.9
kielbasa,* 1 oz	8.0
kiwi fruit, 1 item	0.3
knockwurst,* 1 oz	7.9
kohlrabi, 1 c	0.2
Kool-aid, 1 c	0.0
kumquat, 1 item	0.0

L

LAMB: *listed in three ounce portions. Three ounces of lamb is about 3 inches by 4 inches by 1 inch. The saturated fat in lamb will interfere with heart disease reversal.*

Item	Fat Grams
-leg or shoulder, lean, well-trimmed, braised, 3 oz	12.0
-ground lamb, raw, 3 oz	19.8
-leg, roasted, 3 oz	5.7
-rib, lean, trimmed, broiled, 3 oz	11.0
lard, 1 tbs	13.0
lasagna,* 3x3x1.5"	
-meatless, made with egg white and fat free cheese,* 1 piece	1.0
-meatless,* with regular cheese, 1 piece	13.0
-with meat,* 1 piece	19.0
-with sausage,* 1 piece	29.0

Item	Fat Grams
leeks, 1 c	0.4
lemon, 1 item	0.3
lemon peel, 1 tbs	0.0
lemonade, from frozen concentrate, 6 fluid oz	0.1
lentils, boiled, 1 c	0.7
lettuce	
-iceburg, 1 c	0.1
-Romaine, 1 c	0.2
licorice, 1 stick	0.0
lima beans, dried and then boiled, 1 c .	0.7
lima beans, fresh, 1 c	0.6
lime, 1 item	0.1
limeade, from concentrate, 6 fluid oz	0.1
liquor and liqueurs, clear, 1 oz	0.0
liquor and liqueurs, creamy, 1 oz	2.0
liver, beef, 1 oz	1.0
liver, chicken, 1 oz	1.0
liver, pork, 1 oz	1.0
liverwurst,* 1 oz	8.0
lobster, 3.5 oz	1.9
M	
macadamia nuts,* 10-12 pieces	21.7
macaroni, plain, 1 c	1.0
macaroni and cheese*	
-from scratch,* 1 c	22.2
-from mix,* 1 c varies, see label,	5.0-19.0
-unprepared mix,* 1.8 oz varies, read label	1.0-12.0
-canned or frozen* 1 c	10.0
-made with fat free cheese and no added fat,* 1 c	1.0
mackerel, canned,* 1 c	12.0
malted milk, regular, 1c	17.6
malted milk, soft serve, 1 c	12.0
mandarin oranges, 1/2 c	0.1
mango, 1 medium	0.6
maple syrup, 1 tbs	0.0

* high in sodium   **If there is fat in the ingredient list, there will be a trace of fat in fat free foods

Item	Fat Grams
margarine*: rely on product label	
-regular, 1 tsp	4.0
-diet, 1 tsp	2.0
-fat free, 1 tbs	0.2-0.4
marinara sauce,* vegetarian	
-traditional, 1 c	8.0
-no added fat, 1 c	0.0
marshmallow, 1 item	0.0
marshmallow sauce, 1/2 c	0.0
mashed potatoes	
-traditional, 1/2 c	4.0
-no added fat, 1/2 c	trace
matzo, 6", 3 crackers	1.0
matzo ball, 2", 1 ball	8.0
mayonnaise*	
-regular, 1 tbs	11.0
-low-fat, 1 tbs	4.0
-fat free, 1 tbs	trace
meatball,* traditional, 2" 1 item	15.0
meatloaf,* 4.5x2.5x.5", 1 slice	16.0
melba toast, plain, 4	0.5
melon	
-casaba, 1 c	0.2
-cantaloupe, 1 c	0.5
-honeydew, 1 c	0.2
-watermelon, 1 c	0.7
melon balls, 1 c	0.4
milk:	
-skim, 1 c	0.4
-1/2%, 1 c	1.0
-1%, 1 c	2.6
-2%, 1 c	4.7
-whole, 1 c	8.0
-powdered milk, 1/3 c	0.1
milk, chocolate flavored (made with syrup)	
-regular, 1 c	8.3
-low-fat, 1 c	5.0
-skim, 1c	0.5

Item	Fat Grams
milk, buttermilk* *rely on label*	
-skim,* 1 c	0.4
-cultured,* 1 c	2.2
milk, condensed, sweetened,* 1 c	26.6
milk, evaporated*	
-skim, 1 c	0.6
-regular, 1 c	19.0
milk shake, ice cream, 1 c	17.6
milk shake, soft serve, 1 c	12.0
millet, 1 c	2.0
mincemeat,* 1/3 c	2.0
miso,* 1 oz	1.7
mixed fruit, frozen, 1 c	1.1
mixed fruit, dried, 3.5 oz	0.5
mixed vegetables, frozen, 1 c	0.2
molasses, 1/2 c	0.3
mozzarella cheese*	
-regular,* 1 oz	7.0
-part skim,* 1 oz	4.5
-fat free,* 1 oz	trace
muffins,* 3", diameter	
-from mix,* 1 item	4.0
-with streusel,* 1 item	6.0
-bakery,* 1 item	10.0
-homemade,* 1 item	4.0
muffins, English, 1 whole	1.0
mulberries, 1 c	0.6
mungbeans, sprouted, 1/2 c	0.1
mushrooms, cooked, 1 c	0.8
mustard*	
-yellow, 1 tbs	0.7
-brown, 1 tbs	1.0
-with mustard seeds, 1 tbs	3.0
mustard seed oil, 1 tbs	14.0
mustard greens, 1 c	0.4

N

Item	Fat Grams
navy beans,1 c	1.0
nectarine, 1 medium	0.6

* high in sodium   **If there is fat in the ingredient list, there will be a trace of fat in fat free foods

Item	Fat Grams
New England clam chowder*	
-with cream,* 1 c	36.0
-with whole milk,* 1 c	6.0
-with skim milk,* 1 c	3.4
New England sausage, 1 oz	2.0
noodles:	
-spaghetti, macaroni, 1 c	1.0
-egg noodles, 1 c	2.0
-kluski, 1 c	3.0
-noodles, chow mein,* 1 c	11.0
Noodles Romanoff,* 1 c	24.0
nut bread,* 4.5x2.5x.5", 1 slice	10.0
nutmeg, 1 tsp	0.8
nuts (most*) 1/4 c	16.0-19.0
nuts (most*) 1 oz	15.0
-almonds, 1/4 c	17.8
-brazil nuts, 1/4 c	23.0
-cashews, 1/4 c	15.9
-chestnuts, water, 1/2 c	0.1
-coconut, shredded, 1/4 c	7.0
-hazelnuts, (filberts) 1/4 c	23.9
-peanuts, 1/4 c	18.0
-pecans, 1/4 c	17.5
-pine nuts, 1/4 c	20.3
-pistachio nuts ,1/4 c	16.9
-walnuts, 1/4 c	19.0

O

Item	Fat Grams
oatbran cereal, 1 c cooked	2.5
oatmeal, 1 c cooked	2.0
oatmeal bread, 1 slice	1.2
oatmeal, instant-read product label, varies greatly depending on flavor	
oil, most kinds, 1 tbs	14.0
okra, 1 c	0.2
olives,* green or black, 1 med	0.4
olive oil, 1 tbs	14.0
omelet, 2 egg, plain:	
-cooked, with fat	19.0
-cooked, with no fat	11.0

Item	Fat Grams
omelet,* 2 egg, cheese:	
-cooked, with fat*	25.0
-cooked, without fat*	18.0
omelet, 4 egg whites, plain	
-cooked, with fat	8.0
-cooked, without fat	0.0
onion, 1 c	0.4
onion rings,* fried, 6 rings	11.0
orange juice, fresh, 1 c	0.5
orange juice, from concentrate, 1 c	0.1
orange, navel, 1 medium	0.1
orange, Valencia, 1 medium	0.4
orange peel, 1 tbs	0.0
orange roughy, 3.5 oz	7.0
oysters, 5 to 8 medium	2.2
oyster crackers,* 10 crackers	1.0

P

Item	Fat Grams
pancake,* 4", traditional 1 cake	3.0
pancake,* fat modified, 1 cake	1.0
pancake,* potato, 4", 1 cake	7.0
papaya, 1 medium	0.4
parmesan cheese*	
-regular,* 1 tbs	1.9
-reduced fat* 1 tbs	1.0
-fat free,* 1 tbs**	trace
parsley, 1/2 c	0.1
parsnips,1 c	0.4
PASTA: read label and ingredient list to determine presence of fat	
-macaroni, spaghetti, 1 c	1.0
-egg based, fettuccini, 1 c	2.0
-kluski, 1 c	3.0
pastrami,* lean, beef, 1 oz	1.0
pastrami,* lean turkey, 1 oz	1.0
pastry, Danish, 3x3", 1 piece	13.8
Payday nut roll, 1.8 oz	14.0
pate*	
-chicken liver, 1 oz	4.0
-goose liver, 1 oz	12.0
-beef liver, 1 oz	8.0

* high in sodium   **If there is fat in the ingredient list, there will be a trace of fat in fat free foods

Item	Fat Grams
peas, green 1 c	0.6
pea pods, 1 c	0.6
peach, 1 medium	0.1
peaches, canned or frozen, 1 c	0.3
peanuts, 1/4 c	18.0
peanut butter,* 1 tbs	8.0
peanut butter,* reduced fat, 1 tbs	7.0
peanut butter cups,* 1.6 oz	15.0
pear, 1 large	0.7
pears, canned, 1 c	0.3
peas, dried, 1/2 c	0.8
peas, fresh, 1/2 c	0.6
peas, split, 1/2 c	0.8
pecans, 1/4 c	17.5
pepper, black, 1/4 tsp	0.0
peppers, fresh bell, 1/2 c chopped	0.2
pepper steak,* 1 c	10.0
pepperoni,* 1 oz	12.0
perch, 3.5 oz	1.2
pheasant, with skin 1 oz	7.0
pheasant, without skin 1 oz	3.0
picante sauce,* 1 oz	0.0
pickerel, 3.5 oz	0.5
pickle relish, sweet, 1 tbs	0.0
pickles,* 1 item	0.0
pie, traditional pie recipe, 9" round	
-single crust, cream, 1/8th pie	15.0
-single crust, fruit, 1/8th pie	9.0
-single crust, nut, 1/8th	32.0
-double crust, fruit ,1/8th pie	18.0
pie, fruit pie, tart, 1 item	23.0
pie crust without filling, traditional crust recipe, 9" round	
-single crust, 1/8th pie	9.0
-double crust, 1/8th pie	18.0
pie crust, graham cracker, 1/8th pie	5.0-8.0
pig's feet,* pickled, 1 foot	14.0
pike, 3.5 oz	1.2
pimientos, canned 1 oz	0.1
pineapple, raw 1 c	0.7
pineapple, canned 1 c	0.3

Item	Fat Grams
pineapple juice, 6 ounces	0.2
pine nuts, 1/4 c	20.3
pinto beans, cooked, 1 c	0.9
pistachio nuts,1/4 c	16.9
pita bread, 1 loaf, white	0.7
pita bread, 1 loaf, whole wheat	1.7
pizza,* 14" round, cheese:	
-thin crust, 1/8th pie	10.0
-thick crust, 1/8th pie	13.0
pizza,* pepperoni: use above, but add 12 grams for each ounce of pepperoni eaten.	
plantain, 1 c	0.3
plum, 1 item	0.4
plum sauce, 1/4 c	0.0
poi, 1/2 c	0.2
Polish sausage,* 3 oz	24.0
pomegranate, 1 medium	0.5
popcorn:*	
-air popped, salted, plain 1c	0.5
-air popped, buttered, 1 c	8.5
-popped with oil, salted, plain 1 c	2.0
-popped with oil, buttered, 1 c	10.0
-microwaved: rely on label	
poppy seed, 1 tsp	1.3
popsicle	0.0

PORK: note values are generally listed per one ounce. An average pork chop weighs between 3 and 6 ounces. The saturated fat in pork interferes with heart disease reversal.

-bacon,* 1 slice	3.0
-Canadian, bacon,* 1 oz	2.0
-fresh pork, untrimmed, 1 oz	6.0
-fresh pork, lean, 1 oz	4.0
-ground pork, 1 oz	7.0
-tenderloin, lean, 1 oz	1.0
pork: ham*	
-untrimmed* 1 oz	4.0
-lean,* 1 oz	3.0
-boiled,* 1 oz	3.0
-deviled, canned,* 1 oz (2tbs.)	6.0

* high in sodium   **If there is fat in the ingredient list, there will be a trace of fat in fat free foods

Item	Fat Grams
pork sausage*	
-brown and serve,* 1 oz	3.0-6.0
-bulk, fresh, 1 oz	9.0
-Vienna links,* 2", 1 link	4.0
pork liver, 1 oz	1.0
pork hock,* pickled, 1 foot	14.0
pork ribs, 1 oz	9.0
pork, salt pork,* 1 oz	20.0
pork and beans,* 1 c	3.0-4.6
pot pie* frozen-rely on label	
-beef,* 1 item	24.0
-chicken,* 1 item	24.0
-tuna,* 1 item	18.0
-turkey,* 1 item	23.0
-pot pie, home made* beef, chicken, or turkey, 1 item	31.0
potato, fresh, 1 item	0.1
potato flour, 1 c	1.4
potato chips,* 1 c (13 chips)	10.0
potato pancake,* 4", 1 item	7.0
potato salad,* creamy	
-with mayonnaise, 1/2 c	15.0
-with miracle whip, 1/2 c	9.0
-with non-fat mayo, 1/2 c	trace
potatoes, au gratin,* 1/2 c	7.0
potatoes, French fried*	
-fast food, small serving*	10.0
-fast food, large serving*	22.0
-restaurant, 1 c*	6.0
-homemade, 1 c*	4.9
potatoes, fried,* 1/2 c	4.0
potatoes, hash brown, 1/2 c	10.9
potatoes, mashed	
-traditional, 1/2 c	4.0
-no added fat, 1/2 c	trace
potatoes, scalloped,* 1/2 c	4.0
potatoes, sweet, 1 c	1.0
potatoes, Tater Tots,* 6 tots	5.0
prawns, 2 (1 oz. each)	1.0
preserves, jams, 1 tbs	<0.1

Item	Fat Grams
pressed meat,* 1 oz	1.0
pretzels,* 1 oz	1.0
prunes, dried, 10 items	0.4
prunes, canned, 5 items	0.2
prune juice, 1 c	0.1
pudding, packaged	
-with whole milk, 1/2 c	4.0
-with skim milk, 1/2 c	trace
pudding, rice, packaged	
-with whole milk, 1/2 c	5.0
-with skim milk, 1/2 c	1.0
pumpkin, fresh, 1 c	0.2
pumpkin seeds, plain, 1/4 c	7.0

Q

quail	
-with skin, 1 oz	7.0
-without skin, 1 oz	3.0
quiche,* traditional, 9", 1/8th of pie	14.0
quince, 1 medium	0.1

R

rabbit, 1 oz	2.0
radish, 10 items	0.2
radicchio,1 c	0.2
raisins, 2/3 c	0.5
raisins, yogurt coated, 1 oz	5.5
Ralston hot cereal, 1 c cooked	1.0
Ramen* noodles, 1 c	8.6
Ramen* noodles, low fat, 1 c	0.7
raspberries, 1 c	0.7
ratatouille* traditional recipe, 1 c	15.0
ravioli,* meat	
-canned,* 7.5 oz	4.6
-frozen,* 5 oz	5.7
red beans, 1 c	0.9
red snapper, 3.5 oz	1.9
refried beans*	
-made with fat,* 1/2 c	13.0
-canned,* 1/2 c	2.0
-mashed pinto beans, 1/2 c	0.5

* high in sodium   **If there is fat in the ingredient list, there will be a trace of fat in fat free foods

Item	Fat Grams
relish, pickle, 1 tbs	0.0
rice bran, one ounce	6.2
rice flour, 1 c	0.9
rice, white, 1 c	0.5
rice, brown, 1 c	1.8
rice, wild, 1 c	0.6
rice, fried,* no meat, 1 c	15.0
rice pilaf* made with fat, 1 c	15.0
rice, Spanish,* no meat, 1 c	3.0
rice cake, 1 item	0.3
rice krispie bar, 2x1"	1.0
rice mixes,* seasoned	
-prepared with fat, 1 c	9.0
-prepared without fat, 1 c	1.0
rice pudding, traditional, 1 c	5.0
ricotta cheese	
-regular, 1/2 c	16.0
-part skim, 1/2 c	10.0
-fat free, 1 oz	trace
Ritz crackers,* 4 crackers	3.0
roast beef sandwich	
-cafeteria, with mayo, 1 item	21.0
-fast food, 1 item	16.0
roll, hard or dinner, 1 roll	2.0
rusk, 1 cracker	1.0
rutabaga, 1 c	0.4
Rycrisp, 3 whole	1.0
rye bread, 1 slice	0.9
rye flour, dark, 1 c	3.3
rye flour, light, 1 c	1.0

S

Item	Fat Grams
salad dressings*: rely on product label	
-miracle whip, 1 tbs	7.0
-miracle whip, low-fat 1 tbs	5.0
-clear dressings, regular 1 tbs	7.0
-creamy, 1 tbs	6.0
-fat free,** 1 tbs	0.0-0.4
(if fat is in ingredient list, there will be a trace of fat)	

Item	Fat Grams
salami*	
-cooked, 1 oz	6.0
-hard, 1 oz	10.0
salmon—(see fish)	
-fresh, Atlantic, 3.5 ounces	6.3
-canned,* pink, 1 oz	2.0
-canned,* red, 1 oz	3.0
salmon patty,* 3.5 oz	12.0
salmon rice loaf,* 1 slice	8.0
salsa,* 1/2 c	0.0
salt,* 1 tsp	0.0
salt pork,* 1 oz	20.0
saltine crackers,* 2 squares	0.8
sardines* in oil (drained) 2 items	2.8
sauces	
-barbecue, 3 tbs	1.5
-chili,* 1 tbs	1.0
-Hollandaise,* 1 tbs	7.0
-hot,* (tabasco), 1 tbs	0.0
-steak,* 1 tbs	0.2
-taco,* 1 tbs	0.3
-teriyaki,* 1 tbs	0.0
-Worcestershire,* 1 tbs	0.0
sauces, ice cream	
-caramel, 3 tbs	3.0
-butterscotch, 3 tbs	3.0
-chocolate syrup, 2 tbs	0.3
-fudge sauce, 1 tbs	2.8
sauerkraut,* 1 c	0.4
sausage	
-brown and serve,* 1 oz	3.0-6.0
-bulk, 1 oz	9.0
-bratwurst,* 1 oz	8.0
-Italian,* 1 oz	7.0
-knockwurst,* 1 oz	8.0
-New England,* 1 oz	2.0
-Polish,* 1 oz	8.0
-pork patty, 1 oz	9.0
-Vienna 2',* 1 link	4.0

* high in sodium   **If there is fat in the ingredient list, there will be a trace of fat in fat free foods

Item	Fat Grams
seaweed-most fresh seaweeds for 3.5 oz	0.3-0.6
seaweed, dried spirulina,* 3.5 oz	7.7
scallops, 3.5 oz	1.2
Scramblers, fat free, 1 c	0.0
Second Nature, fat free, 1 c	0.0
seeds: plain	
-pumpkin, 1/4 c	7.0
-sesame, 1 tbs	4.0
-sunflower, 1/4 c	18.0
Shake and Bake™ coating, 1/4 pouch	
-barbeque for pork	1.7
-chicken	1.7
-fish	1.3
-Italian	1.1
-pork	1.1
shakes:	
-ice cream ,1 c	17.6
-soft serve, 1 c	12.0
sherbet, 1/2 c	2.0
shallots, 1 tbs chopped	0.0
shortening 1 tbs	12.0
shrimp ,3.5 oz	1.8
shrimp, salad*:	
-with mayonnaise, 1/2 c	15.0
-with Miracle Whip, 1/2 c	9.0
-with non-fat mayo,1/2 c	2.0
skim milk, 1 c	0.4
sloppy joe on bun*	13.5
sloppy joe "Manwich" sauce,* 1/4 c	0.0
Snicker bar, 2.0 oz	13.0
soda crackers,* 2 squares	0.8
soft drinks, 12 oz	0.0
sole, 3.5 oz	0.5
souffle,* 1 c	18.0
soup*:	
-bean,* no meat, 1 c	2.0
-bean,* with meat, 1 c	6.0
-broth,* strained, defatted, 1 c	0.0

Item	Fat Grams
soups*: broth based , traditional recipes	
-vegetable beef,* 1 c	3.0
-chicken noodle,* 1 c	3.0
-chicken rice,* 1 c	3.0
-Manhattan clam chowder,* 1 c	2.9
-fat strained, vegetarian,* 1 c	trace
soup,* cheese	
-with whole milk,* 1 c	15.0
-with skim milk,* 1 c	11.0
soups,* creamy: tomato, potato, clam chowder	
-with whole milk,* 1 c	6.0
-with skim milk,* 1 c	3.4
-with water,* 1 c	3.0
soups,* creamy: chicken, celery, mushroom	
-whole milk,* 1 c	11.0
-with skim,* milk1 c	8.0
sour cream, regular, 1 tbs	3.0
sour cream, fat free, 1 tbs	trace
soy sauce,* 1 tbs	0.0
soy oil, 1 tbs	14.0
soy protein: rely on label, products vary	
soy protein, textured fat free, 3 tbs	0.0
soybeans, 1/2 c	7.7
soybean flour, defatted, 1 c	1.2
soybean flour, full fat, 1 c	17.6
spaghetti noodles, 1 c	1.0
spaghetti* sauce, traditional commercial	
-with meat,* 1 c	23.0
-without meat,* 1 c	10.0
spaghetti sauce,* canned: rely on label	
spaghetti sauce,* homemade, meatless, no cheese, no oil 1 c	trace
spanakopita,* 3x2" piece, 1	24.0
Spanish rice,* no meat, 1 c	3.0
spices ,1 tsp	0.0
spinach, 1 c cooked	0.4
spinach raw, chopped 1 c	0.2
split peas, 1 c	0.8

* high in sodium   **If there is fat in the ingredient list, there will be a trace of fat in fat free foods

The "Life Tastes Better Than Steak" Eating Plan

Item	Fat Grams
split pea soup*	
-meatless,* 1 c	1.0
-with meat,* 1 c	6.0
squash, summer, 1 c	0.2
squash, winter, 1 c	1.2
steak sauce,* 1 tbs	0.2
stew,* beef	
-with trimmed meat, 1 c	8.0
-untrimmed meat, 1 c	18.0
stewed tomatoes,* 1c	0.4
strawberries, 1c	0.6
stuffing,* traditional, 1/2 c	12.8
stuffing,* package mix, 1/2 c	3.0-8.8
sugar, 1 tbs	0.0
sunflower oil, 1 tbs	14.0
sunflower seeds, 1/4 c	18.0
sweet and sour sauce, 1/4 c	0.0
sweet potato, mashed, plain, 1 c	1.0
sweet roll, Danish	13.8
sweet roll, cinnamon	9.3
sweetener, artificial, 1 tsp	0.0
Swiss cheese*	
-regular,* 1 oz	7.8
-processed,* 1 oz	7.1
-low fat,* 1 oz	3.0
-fat free,* 1oz	trace
Swiss steak, meat only	
-untrimmed, 1 oz	2.0
-trimmed, 1 oz	1.0
Syrup	
-chocolate, 2 tbs	0.3
-maple, 2 tbs	0.0
-pancake, 2 tbs	0.0

T

Item	Fat Grams
Tabasco sauce,* 1 tsp	0.0
tabbouleh, traditional, 1/2 c	9.0
taco,* fast food, beef, 1 item	10.0
taco sauce,* 1 tbs	0.3

Item	Fat Grams
taco shell, not fried	
-flour, plain, 1 med	2.0
-corn, plain, 1 med	1.0
tamale*:	
-meat, no cheese, 1 item	6.0
-meat and cheese, 1 item	8.0
tangerine, 1 item	0.2
tapioca pudding, 1/2 c	5.0
taro, 1/2 c	0.1
tartar sauce, 1 tbs	9.0
tarts, fruit pie tarts, 1 item	23.0
Tater tots,* 6 tots	5.0
tea, 1 c	0.0
teriyaki sauce,* 1 tbs	0.0
three bean salad,* traditional, 1/2 c	11.0
toaster pop tarts, 1 item	16.0
tofu, frozen, 1/2 c	12.0
tofu, raw	
-regular, 1 oz	1.0
-regular, 1/2 c	6.0
-firm, 1 oz	2.0
-firm, 1/2 c	11.0
-silken lite firm, 3 ounces	1.0
tomato, red or green, 1 item	0.3
tomato juice,* 3/4 c	0.1
tomato products, canned*	
-tomato paste,* 1 c	2.0
-tomato sauce,* 1 c	0.3
-tomatoes, stewed,* 1 c	0.4
toppings, for ice cream	
-caramel or butterscotch syrup, 3 tbs	3.0
-fudge sauce, 1 tbs	3.0-5.0
-chocolate syrup, 2 tbs	2.8
-pineapple topping, 3 tbs	0.3
-strawberry sauce, 3 tbs	0.1
tortilla, not fried	
-corn, plain 1	1.0
-flour, plain 1	2.0
-fat free, corn or flour	trace
-extra large, flour	4.0

* high in sodium   **If there is fat in the ingredient list, there will be a trace of fat in fat free foods

"A Diet for a Clogged Artery"

♥ ♥ ♥

Item	Fat Grams
tortilla chips,* 1 c	5.0
tossed salad, plain, 1 c	0.1
trout, brook, 3.5 oz	2.1
trout, lake, 3.5 oz	6.5
trout, rainbow, 3.5 oz	1.2

TUNA*: *canned, read label because there can be a wide range of fat grams, depending on the type of tuna. Water packed tuna is not always lowfat.*

Item	Fat Grams
tuna,* canned light, in oil, 3.5 oz	8.1
tuna,* canned light, in water, 3.5 oz	2.4
tuna,* canned, white, in oil, 3.5 oz	8.0
tuna,* canned, white, in water, 3.5 oz	2.4
tuna, fresh albacore, 3.5 oz	7.5
tuna, fresh bluefin, 3.5 oz	4.1
tuna, fresh yellowfin, 3.5 oz	3.0
tuna salad*	
-with mayonnaise, 1/2 c	22.0
-with miracle whip, 1/2 c	17.0
-fat free mayo, water packed, 1/2 c	1.0
tuna patty, traditional,* 3.5 oz	11.0

TURKEY: *amounts are for one ounce. Most turkey portions are three to eight ounces*

Item	Fat Grams
-white meat & skin, 1 oz	3.0
-white meat, no skin, 1 oz	1.0
-dark meat & skin, 1 oz	4.0
-dark meat, no skin, 1 oz	2.0
turkey, diced with no skin	
-white, 1/2 c	3.0
-dark, 1/2 c	6.0
-white dark mixed, 1/2 c	4.0
turkey, ground	
-white dark mixed, with skin, 1 oz	4.0
-white, no skin, 1 oz	1.0
turkey, ground, cooked, rinsed with hot water, 1 oz	1.0
turkey ham,* lean, 1 oz	1.0
turkey roll,* 1 oz	2.0
turnip, 1 c, cubed	0.2
turnip greens, 1 c cooked	0.4
turnover, fruit, 1 item	15.0

U

Item	Fat Grams
unprocessed wheat bran, 1 tbs	0.1

V

VEAL: *amounts are for one ounce. Most veal dishes contain four to six ounces*

Item	Fat Grams
-breast or rib, 1 oz	6.0
-ground veal, 1 oz	2.0
-loin cuts, lean, 1 oz	2.0
-loin cuts, untrimmed, 1 oz	4.0
-leg, shoulder, lean, 1 oz	3.0
-leg, shoulder, untrimmed, 1 oz	2.0
vegetable oil cooking spray	
-regular, 1 second of spray	1.0
-reduced fat, 1 second of spray	0.5
vegetable juice cocktail,* 1 c	0.2
venison, 1 oz	1.0
Vienna sausage,* 2", 1 link	4.0
vinegar, 1/2 c	0.0
Vitamin E, 800 I.U.S.	0.8

W-Z

Item	Fat Grams
waffle,* 7", traditional, 1 item	14.0
Waldorf salad:*	
-with mayonnaise, 1/2 c	19.0
-with miracle whip, 1/2 c	13.0
-with fat free mayonnaise, no whipping cream and no nuts 1/2 c	trace
walnuts, 1/4 c	19.0
watermelon, 1 c	0.7
wax beans, 1 c	0.4
welsh rarebit,* 1 c	32.0
wheat bread, 100% wholewheat, 1 slice	1.0
wheat bran, 1 oz	1.0
wheat flour, bread or high gluten, 1 c	3.0
wheat flour, white all purpose, 1 c	1.0
wheat flour, whole grain, 1 c	2.0
wheat germ, 1 tbs	1.0
Wheat thins,* 3 crackers	1.0

* high in sodium   **If there is fat in the ingredient list, there will be a trace of fat in fat free foods

The "Life Tastes Better Than Steak" Eating Plan

♥ ♥ ♥

Item	Fat Grams
WHIPPED TOPPING: note — most contain highly saturated fat such as palm or coconut oil or hydrogenated fats. Read the serving size on the label. Products with these fats will interfere with reversal.	
-from mix, 1 tbs	0.5
-frozen, 1 tbs	1.0
-Cool Whip, 1 tbs	0.8
-Cool Whip Light, 2 tbs	0.5
-Cool Whip Free, 2 tbs	<0.5
-Kraft Free, 2 tbs	<0.5
whipped cream, 1 tbs	0.3
whipping cream, heavy cream, 1 tbs	5.6
whitefish, 3.5 oz	5.8
white beans, 1 c cooked	0.6
white sauce, whole milk, 1/4 c	9.0
white sauce, skim milk, 1/4 c	7.0
white sauce made with skim milk and no added fat, 1/4 c	0.1
whiting, 3.5 oz	1.7

Item	Fat Grams
whole wheat flour, 1 c	2.0
Whopper,* 1 item	36.0
Whopper with cheese,* 1 item	44.0
Whopper,* double with cheese	61.0
wild rice, 1 c	0.6
wine, 4 oz	0.0
wonton,* 1.75", 1 item	4.0
Worcestershire sauce,* 1 tbs	0.0
yam, cooked, 1/2 c	0.1
yeast, brewer's, 1 tbs	0.0
yellow beans, dried and then boiled 1 c	1.9
yellowtail fish, 3.5 oz	5.4
yogurt	
-whole milk, 1 c	8.0
-low-fat (1-2%), 1 c	3.0
-fat free, 1 c	0.4
yogurt, frozen, low-fat, 1 c	3.0
yogurt, frozen, fat free, 1 c	trace
zwieback,1 item	1.0